Indust

This is the *essential* resource for publishers and authors!

"Full of resources for selling Christian books. **Incredibly useful.**"
John Kremer, Author
1001 Ways to Market Your Books

"An absolute **'must-have'** for anyone involved in marketing Christian books, though the general tips, tricks, and techniques will prove useful for marketing mainstream books as well."
Jim Cox
Midwest Book Review

"This well-organized book is just brimming with marketing ideas and resources specifically for the author seeking a Christian audience. This book could make the difference between a mediocre and a **WOW** promotions campaign."
Patricia Fry, President
SPAWN

"Sarah Bolme understands the shades of difference that separate the Christian market from the secular alternatives. She adroitly covers all the essential bases—promotion, publicity, distribution, special sales and traditional marketing. Her detailed contact listings are the golden nuggets that give the book its **unfathomable value**. An author or publisher armed with this expert guide would have to try hard not to succeed.

"I now have valuable information I had not seen anywhere else, and I've been involved in Christian publishing for over seven years. Every Christian author and publisher needs this book."
Debbie Thurman
Cedar House Publishers

"Thanks again for the great book you wrote! It is very well written and easy to understand. The information is **priceless**."
Grace Bass
A&B Publishing

"The most common cause of books not doing well is the lack of good marketing. Sarah's book does a **great job of guiding** authors and publishers in making sure they build consumer and trade awareness and demand for their book."

Larry Carpenter, industry veteran
Christian Book Services

"Thank you for your wonderful book about Christian Book Marketing. **What a lifesaver** it has been. You gave me so many ideas and resources that I had never even imagined before. I can't thank you enough for such a great resource!"

Leslie Nelson, author

"*Your Guide to Marketing Books in the Christian Marketplace* is the **BEST SELF HELP BOOK** that I have come across, and I have read most all of them, including Dan Poynter's. Everything is laid out with ease and extraordinary flow."

Deborah Slappey Pitts, Publisher
Harobed House

"The **best Christian marketing book** I have read! I love this book. I especially like the fact that you provide information on Urban marketing. As an African-American author, I find the 'Targeting Special Markets' section a priceless gem."

Mary Ann Battle
Publisher

"Sarah removes the scariness of the unknown and replaces it with the specific knowledge you need to market your book for the Christian audience, and the encouragement to persevere.

"Bethany Press is excited to have this **valuable resource** for our customers! We believe that it will provide them with the practical information they need to succeed."

Sara Rosenberg
Bethany Press

Your Guide to
MARKETING
Books in the
CHRISTIAN MARKETPLACE

3rd Edition

Sarah Bolme
CREST Publications
Charlotte, NC

Your Guide to Marketing Books in the Christian Marketplace, 3rd Edition
Copyright © 2006–2014 by Sarah Bolme

All rights reserved. No part of this book may be reproduced or transmitted in any form or by any means, electronic or mechanical, including photocopying, recording, or saving on any information storage and retrieval system, without permission in writing from the publisher.
    Crest Publications and the shield logo are trademarks of Crest Publications.
    All scripture quotations are taken from the Holy Bible New International Version® NIV®, Copyright © 1973, 1978, 1984 by International Bible Society. Used with permission.

Notice of Liability

The information in this book is distributed on an "as is" basis, without warranty. While every precaution has been taken in the preparation of the book, neither the author nor Crest Publications shall have any liability to any person or entity with respect to any loss or damage caused or alleged to be caused directly or indirectly by the instructions contained in this book.
    Internet addresses and contact information printed in this book are offered as a resource to you. These are not intended in any way to be or imply an endorsement on the part of Crest Publications, nor do we vouch for the content of these sites and numbers for the life of this book.

ISBN: 978-0-9725546-9-5

Library of Congress Control Number: 2013922944

Printed in the United States of America
First Edition: 2006
Second Edition: 2009
Third Edition: 2014

Cover design: Kalissa Fitzgerald
Interior design: Edward Bolme / Crest Publisher Services

Published by: Crest Publications
PO Box 481022
Charlotte, NC 28269
www.marketingchristianbooks.com
www.crestpub.com

*To my wonderful husband, Edward,
without whose continued loving support
and encouragement this book would not exist.*

Table of Contents

Foreword 1
Introduction 3

Part One: Launching Your Books

1: Get Connected 7
    Join a Publishers Association 8
    Subscribe to Industry Publications 12
    Join Online Discussion Groups 14
    Connections for Christian Authors 14
    Summary 17
2: Gather Endorsements 19
    The Benefits of Endorsements 20
    Securing Endorsements 21
    Use of Endorsements 21
    Summary 21
3: Secure Distribution 23
    Types of Distribution 24
    Christian Wholesale Book Companies 26
    General Market Wholesale Book Companies 27
    Christian Marketplace Distributors 28
    Distribution for Print-on-Demand Titles 30
    Summary 31

4: Announce Your Books......33
    Trade Announcements......34
    General Announcements......37
    Summary......39
5: Garner Book Reviews......41
    Materials to Include When Requesting a Review......42
    Christian Trade Reviews......43
    General Trade Reviews......44
    Reviews for Church Librarians......47
    Reviews for Christian Consumers......49
    Online Christian Book Review Sites......50
    After a Review......53
    Summary......53
6: Host a Book Launch Event......55
    Physical Event......56
    Virtual Event......58
    Summary......60

Part Two: Selling Your Books

7: Pursue Book Awards......63
    Christian Book Awards......65
    General Book Awards with Religious Categories......68
    Summary......72
8: Reach Christian Retailers......73
    BISAC......75
    Industry Trade Shows......75
    Advertisements in Trade Journals......77
    Promotion Through Retail Marketing Groups......78
    Advertising Through Your Distributor......81
    Direct Mail Campaigns......81
    Direct Sales......83
    Online Christian Bookstores......85
    Summary......86
9: Connect with Churches......87
    Church Libraries......88
    Church Leaders......89
    Direct Mail......93
    Email Blasts......94
    Advertising in Magazines and Journals......94
    Creative Marketing......95
    Summary......95

10: Partner with Christian Organizations 97
    Mail-Order Catalogs. 98
    Christian Charities 100
    Christian Organizations. 101
    Christians in the Military 102
    Christian Schools 105
    Christian Camps and Conference Centers 112
    Creative Marketing. 114
    Summary 115
11: Engage Christian Media 117
    Christian Magazines. 118
    Christian Newspapers 120
    Christian Radio and Television. 124
    Local Radio Stations. 128
    Christian Television Networks 129
    Summary 130
12: Access Christian Consumers 131
    Author Book Signings 132
    Author Speaking Engagements. 134
    Market Your Books to Reading Groups. 137
    Promote Your Books at Local Book Festivals 139
    Public Libraries 140
    Foreign Rights 142
    Creative Marketing. 142
    Summary 147
13: Harness the Internet. 149
    Create a Website 150
    Advertise Online. 153
    Affiliate Programs. 156
    Conduct Email Campaigns 156
    Create Book Videos 157
    Take a Virtual Book Tour. 160
    Optimize Amazon's Author Central. 162
    BlogTalkRadio. 164
    QR Codes. 166
    Creative Marketing. 167
    Summary 167
14: Leverage Social Networking 169
    Rules of Engagement 170
    Blogs. 171
    Social Network Community Sites. 173

Book Social Networking 178
Join Online Communities 180
A Word of Caution 181
Summary 181
15: Handle Overstocks and Remainders 183
Bargain Book Companies 184
Gifting Books to a Nonprofit Organization 186
Summary 188

Part Three: Targeting Special Markets

16: eBooks 191
Digital Publishing Trade Associations 192
eBook Distribution 193
eBook Subscription Services 197
eBook Awards 198
Promoting Your eBooks to Readers 200
Digital Book Signings 203
The Physical Selling of Digital Books 204
Creative Marketing 205
Summary 205
17: The Homeschool Market 207
Homeschool Associations 208
Distribution 209
Homeschool Magazines 213
Reaching Homeschoolers on the Internet 215
Homeschool Radio Programs 216
Homeschool e-Newsletters 217
Homeschool Conventions 217
Homeschool Direct Mailings 220
Summary 220
18: The Urban Market 221
Urban Christian Distribution 222
Urban Book Reviews 222
Urban Press Release Services 224
Urban Christian Speakers Bureaus 225
Urban Christian Reading Groups 226
Urban Christian Book Clubs 227
Urban Radio and Television 227
African-American Church Denominations 228
Historically Black Colleges and Universities 228

    African-American Homeschoolers 229
    Urban Book Awards 229
    Social Networking for African-American Authors 230
    Summary 230
19: Spanish-Language Books 231
    Spanish-Language Products Association. 232
    Spanish-Language Trade Shows 232
    Spanish-Language Book Reviews. 233
    Spanish-Language Distribution 233
    Spanish-Language Radio and Television. 235
    Spanish-Language Book Awards 236
    Summary 237

Part Four: Reference

Index. 241

About the Author 246
Book Marketing Template. 247
Christian Small Publishers Association. 248
BookCrash. 249
Special Marketing Bonus. 250

Your Guide to
MARKETING
Books in the
CHRISTIAN MARKETPLACE

Foreword

I hear from new book authors all the time whose typical lament is: "I have a book coming out—or my book has come out—but I have no idea what to do to get it out into the marketplace." I'm always looking for good resources to help, and since I deal almost exclusively with Christian authors, I want those resources to reflect the unique needs of that market.

I can't tell you how delighted I was to find *Your Guide to Marketing Books in the Christian Marketplace*. It is not only full of great helps and practical ideas for marketing your own book; it is also a wealth of Christian-oriented resources. Since the job of marketing needs to start long before the book is released, this book will be most helpful to those who are market savvy enough to start the process as soon as the contract is signed. However, if you didn't get started as soon as you should have, you will still find a lot of resources to help you make up for the lost time.

One of the best features of this guide is that it takes you step-by-step through the various aspects of promotion—not just telling you what you should do, but how to find the contacts that will be critical to your success. The listings of organizations, reviewers, consumer groups, and websites alone are worth the price of the book.

I would encourage writers to read through the book first to become aware of all the possibilities for promoting their book, then go back and work through each section applying what looks like it will work for promoting their particular book. It's the application of these tricks of the trade that will make the difference between successful sales and a garage full of unsold books.

One thing that shines through as you read this book is the author's knowledge of the industry. Sarah Bolme has written a book to fill an ongoing need in the industry, based on her years of experience working with authors and small publishers. It's obvious that she's also done her homework to bring you up-to-date resources to make your job easier. You can trust the author and follow the path she has laid out with confidence.

Now, with this tool in hand, you're prepared to launch out into the exciting job that lies ahead.

Sally E. Stuart
Founder
Christian Writers' Market Guide
www.stuartmarket.com

Introduction

*We will shout for joy when you are victorious
and will lift up our banners in the name of our God.
May the Lord grant all your requests.*
—Psalm 20:5

The landscape of publishing and selling books has undergone a monumental shift since I wrote the first edition of *Your Guide to Marketing Books in the Christian Marketplace*. In the past eight years, print-on-demand technology and digital reading have changed the entry barriers for publishing a book.

Today, almost half of all books are self-published. According to Bowker, 40% of all books published in 2012 were self-published. As a result, self-publishing, for the most part, no longer carries the stigma it once did. It is now viewed as a legitimate way to produce a book.

However, the average self-published title still only sells between 40 and 200 copies. Often this is due to the author's inexperience or lack of knowledge on how to market a book effectively. This book is my attempt to help any author who has published a Christian book (whether independently or through a traditional publishing house) and new publishers seeking to reach the Christian market to gain the knowledge necessary to promote books effectively.

Marketing is hard work. It is increasingly difficult to make any book stand out. Each book is competing with more than ten million other books available for sale, while other media is claiming more and more of people's time.

I love this quote by Flannery O'Conner:

> "When a book leaves your hands, it belongs to God. He may use it to save a few souls or to try a few others, but I think that for the writer to worry is to take over God's business."

When promoting the Kingdom of God, getting your books into people's hands is God's business. All you can do is what you know to do. Do that and ask God to bless your feeble efforts. After all, if He can feed over 5,000 people with two small fish and five little loaves of bread, He can multiply your marketing efforts to reach thousands of people, if that is His desire.

Marketing and selling books is not a sprint; it is a marathon. Too many authors give up too quickly when they don't see immediate results. Don't get discouraged. Establishing yourself as a viable resource of quality Christian materials takes time. Many small and self-publishers experience success in the Christian marketplace through perseverance and a comprehensive marketing strategy.

I pray that this book will be a valuable resource to you as you strive to bring new insights and inspiration to the family of God. May God bless you and the books that He leads you to produce to encourage, teach, and equip His people.

His servant,

Sarah Bolme
info@marketingchristianbooks.com

P.S.: As I write this book, it is still largely a print book world. While the sales of digital books are growing, they currently only comprise about 30% of all book sales. Thus, this material is largely written with print books in mind. While all of the marketing advice that follows pertains to both print and digital books, I have kept a chapter specifically for ebooks to deal with some of the special aspects of this format.

Part One

Launching Your Books

Get Connected

*Plans fail for lack of counsel,
but with many advisers they succeed.*
—Proverbs 15:22

> Marketing Fundamental:
> **Information leads to knowledge, which
> leads to wise decisions that bring success.**

Knowledge is vital for success in the publishing and bookselling trade. The industry of publishing and bookselling is in constant motion. What is true today for this business will not necessarily be true next year. Publishers and authors must strive to stay abreast of industry happenings and trends. Knowing your competition and what they are doing is smart business. Understanding the current trends of Christian retail stores and Christian consumers allows you to market your products wisely. The best way to gather the information required to stay up-to-date about this industry is to get connected.

Join a Publishers Association

Name recognition is an essential ingredient in marketing your book in the Christian marketplace. With the myriad of Christian books available today, Christian retailers are inundated with product choices and do not have the time to screen every book they stock in their stores. As a result, most Christian retailers rely on name recognition to ensure that the products they carry contain messages that are consistent with Protestant or Catholic Christian views and are not other religious materials dressed up in Christian attire.

Christian retailers rely on five main sources for name recognition in considering materials for their stores:

- Known Christian author or personality
- Established Christian publishing house
- Endorsement by a known Christian personality
- Favorable review by a reputable Christian source
- Alliance with a Christian publishers association

Since new small and self-publishers are not established Christian publishing houses and typically are not publishing titles by established Christian personalities, pursuing the other three choices are your best options for engendering confidence in the content and quality of your books. An alliance with a Christian publishers association is a good place to start.

Joining a publishers association is a wise decision for any publisher. There are four fundamental benefits of joining a publishers association.

Benefit #1: Respect in the Industry

In the Christian marketplace, name recognition for credibility purposes is probably the most important reason for a new, small, or self-publisher to join a Christian publishers association. Christian retailers gain confidence in a new publisher's products when they know that the publisher is a member of a Christian organization in the industry. Professional organizations hold their members to a higher standard of conduct. Membership in a professional association says, "I am serious about my vocation."

Don't you prefer to go to a doctor who is a member of the American Medical Association? Knowing that your doctor belongs to a professional organization makes you feel more secure that he is serious about learning and knowing the latest medical techniques. As a publisher, your membership in a publishers association brings you the same professional respect in the book industry. For example, book reviews are an essential ingredient in promoting a new title, and membership in a publishers association lends your publishing company credibility with book review sources. One example of this is The Midwest Book Review. This review source specializes in reviewing titles from small publishers, self-publishers, academic publishers, and specialty presses. However, they give priority consideration to those titles from publishers that belong to a publishers association.

Benefit #2: Cutting-Edge Information

Publishers associations provide their members with some form of regular communication (usually a newsletter) containing the latest developments and resources in the publishing industry. Many hold seminars and conferences to further their members' education and expertise in publishing issues. The information you glean from belonging to a publishers association can improve your business and bring you more success in your endeavors. Knowing what is currently working for other publishers helps you learn what to do to sell more copies of your books.

The industry of publishing and bookselling is in constant motion.

Benefit #3: Saving Money

Joining a professional publishers association costs money. However, if you take advantage of the membership benefits these associations offer (which can include discounts on shipping costs, co-op marketing opportunities, health insurance programs for self-employed individuals, and liability insurance), you will save money in the long run. Some small publishers claim that the money they have saved on a freight discount benefit alone more than pays for their annual membership fees in one publishers association.

Benefit #4: Doors of Opportunity

Professional publishers associations provide opportunities for you to network with other professionals in the book industry. Aside from the aforementioned seminars or conferences to attend, some associations also provide an online discussion group for member publishers. These opportunities allow you not only to find out what is working for other publishers but they provide a venue to share your expertise.

Displaying your titles at a trade show can lead to great deals. While trade shows are generally a costly endeavor, some publishers associations provide opportunities for you to display your titles affordably. Some small publishers have sold international rights for their books through displaying titles at the Frankfurt Book Fair through a publishers association.

Publishers Associations

There are currently four professional publishers associations for those publishing materials for the Christian marketplace.

- **Association of Catholic Publishers (ACP)**
  ACP is for publishers producing materials for the Catholic marketplace. This organization has a sliding membership fee based on the size of the publishing house. ACP produces a newsletter, provides co-op marketing opportunities, sponsors seminars, and gives publisher excellence and service awards.
  www.catholicpublishers.org

- **Christian Small Publishers Association (CSPA)**
  CSPA is an organization for small and self-publishers producing materials for the Christian marketplace. CSPA produces an e-newsletter, offers co-op advertising, exhibits members' books at the International Christian Retail Show, offers a distribution program, runs a book review program, and sponsors the Christian Small Publisher Book of the Year Award.
  www.christianpublishers.net

- **Evangelical Christian Publishers Association (ECPA)**
  ECPA is a publishers association for established Christian publishers. It has the highest membership fee of the Christian publishers associations. ECPA considers a small publisher one with annual revenues under one million dollars. To become a member of ECPA, an existing ECPA publisher member must recommend you for membership.
  www.ecpa.org

- **Protestant Church-Owned Publishers Association (PCPA)**
  PCPA is an association of not-for-profit official church-owned Protestant publishing houses, directly connected to their respective denominations. PCPA supports publishers as they serve congregations within their denominations.
  www.pcpaonline.org

Even if you publish only Christian materials, you don't have to limit yourself to Christian publishers associations. Most bookstores and public libraries offer many religious titles for their patrons. Additional membership in a general market publishers association can provide you information and cost-saving marketing opportunities to reach the general book market also.

Here is a list of general market publishers associations for small and self-publishers.

- **Independent Book Publishers Association (IBPA)**
  IBPA publishes a newsletter, sponsors seminars, provides co-op promotional mailings, exhibits members' books at trade conventions, and sponsors the annual Benjamin Franklin Awards for the best books of the year published by independent publishers.
  www.ibpa-online.org

- **The Association of Publishers for Special Sales (APSS)**
  APSS (formerly SPAN) is an association of independent publishers. Their mission is to help publishers sell more books in more ways, primarily by helping their members find new opportunities for profitable sales in non-traditional ways. APSS also operates a free, open, online community for publishers.
  www.bookapss.org

- **Small Publishers, Artists, and Writers Network (SPAWN)**
  SPAWN provides opportunities for everyone involved in publishing. SPAWN encourages the exchange of ideas, information, and other mutual benefits.
  www.spawn.org

- **The Electronic Publishing Industry Coalition (EPIC)**
  EPIC, the Electronic Publishing Industry Coalition, was incorporated in 1998 to provide a strong voice for electronic publishing. Once an authors' organization, EPIC has expanded to include hundreds of professionals from all facets of the electronic publishing industry: authors, publishers, editors, artists, and others.
  www.epicorg.com

- **The Alliance of Independent Authors (ALLI)**
  ALLI is a collaborative collective of independent self-published authors. This association provides advice, encouragement, and networking opportunities for self-published writers.
  www.allianceindependentauthors.org

- **The Independent Author Network (IAN)**
  IAN is a group of self-published authors and authors published by small indie presses who work together to promote each other's books. The group's website includes author pages, an author directory, a bookstore, and social networking for their members.
  www.independentauthornetwork.com

Join as many associations as you feel will optimize the information and opportunities you need to be successful in your publishing endeavors. Once you join a publishers association, make sure to include your membership in that association on your letterhead, your website, your press releases, and all your advertising materials to take full advantage of the name recognition and respect your membership brings you.

Subscribe to Industry Publications

A number of publications help publishers and authors stay abreast of current news and trends in the Christian marketplace. Some of these publications are more costly than others. However, there are a number of free e-newsletters that provide condensed news of the industry for those publishers and authors on a tight budget.

Subscription Publications

You do not need to subscribe to all of these publications to stay abreast of industry conditions. Since the Christian marketplace is a relatively small subset of publishing, information is often repeated between the publications listed here. A subscription to one of these publications complemented with the free e-newsletters listed on the next page is usually sufficient to stay abreast of industry news.

- *Publishers Weekly*
  The most costly of these publications, *Publishers Weekly*, is the preeminent magazine for publishers and booksellers. *Publishers Weekly*

covers the general book publishing market but includes a great deal of information on the religious marketplace.
   www.publishersweekly.com

- **Christian Retailing**
  Produced by Charisma Media (formerly Strang Publications), this magazine has been published for over 50 years. The magazine is free to Christian retail stores, but industry suppliers must pay for the periodical. *Christian Retailing* is produced monthly.
     www.christianretailing.com

- **CBA Retailers + Resources**
  CBA Retailers + Resources is the official publication of CBA, The Association of Christian Retail. This monthly publication is free to all members of CBA. Non-members must pay a subscription fee.
     www.cbaonline.org

Free e-Newsletters

The beauty of e-newsletters is that they are the most cost-effective means of staying abreast of industry news. Most of the subscription publications listed above also offer a weekly e-newsletter free of charge. Simply sign up for the newsletter on each publication's website and you will receive the newsletter each week in your email inbox.

- **Religion BookLine**
  This is *Publishers Weekly*'s e-newsletter providing updates on religion publishing and book buying.
     www.publishersweekly.com

- **Christian Etailing**
  Produced by *Christian Retailing*, this weekly e-newsletter features industry news for the Christian marketplace.
     www.christianretailing.com

- **CBA Retailers + Resources Industry Brief**
  CBA produces this weekly e-newsletter featuring headline news for the Christian publishing and bookselling industry.
     www.cbaonline.org

Join Online Discussion Groups

Joining discussion groups is free and it is a good avenue for acquiring information, ideas, and trends from other publishers. Here is a sampling of online discussion groups for publishers.

- **Christian Self-Publishing**
  This discussion group is for authors and small presses who are involved in self-publishing and marketing material to the homeschooling or Christian private school markets.
  http://groups.yahoo.com/group/ChristianSelf-Publishing

- **Self-Publishing**
  This discussion forum is a community of authors and small presses interested or involved in self-publishing and book marketing for the general marketplace.
  http://finance.groups.yahoo.com/group/self-publishing

- **Publish-L**
  This email discussion group is for issues related to publishing. It is a forum for the exchange of ideas and information about publishing and marketing books to the general marketplace. Anyone interested in publishing or engaged in the industry is welcome.
  www.publish-l.com

- **POD Publishers**
  POD Publishers is a business discussion group for publishers of print-on-demand books. This group is primarily comprised of general market POD publishers.
  http://finance.groups.yahoo.com/group/pod_publishers

Connections for Christian Authors

For Christian authors, staying abreast of the industry is very important for you to promote your books effectively. Keeping informed about industry trends also helps you be aware of the types of materials the marketplace needs so you can be successful in your next writing project. Publishers should encourage their authors to stay connected with other Christian authors in the Christian marketplace. Here are a few ways authors can get connected.

Join a Christian Writers Association

A number of Christian writers associations exist to support, encourage, educate, and inform writers writing for the Christian marketplace.

- **American Christian Fiction Writers Association (ACFW)**
  Membership in ACFW provides Christian writers access to a monthly e-zine, critique groups, mentor groups, access to the ACFW online forum, and promotional opportunities for published authors.
  www.acfw.com

- **American Christian Writers Association (ACW)**
  ACW offers regional writers conferences around the country, regional charters of local writers groups, and two publications: *Christian Communicator* and *Advanced Christian Writer*. Membership in ACW is not required to access any of these great services. Subscriptions are available for the association's two print publications.
  www.acwriters.com

- **Catholic Writers Guild**
  The Catholic Writers Guild is for Catholic writers looking for a group of like-minded writers willing to assist each other in their publishing goals. The organization offers online support and communities.
  www.catholicwritersguild.org

- **Christian Writers Guild**
  Run by Jerry B. Jenkins, membership in this group gives authors access to webinars, manuscript critiques, a novel contest, and writers conferences.
  www.christianwritersguild.com

- **Fellowship of Christian Writers (FCW)**
  Located in Tulsa, Oklahoma, FCW began as a local Christian writers ministry, but is now available to writers at large. Membership provides a monthly newsletter; access to local writers groups featuring speakers, workshops, and critique groups; and entry into their writing contest. FCW also hosts a Yahoo! discussion group that is open to any Christian writer.
  www.fellowshipofchristianwriters.org

Attend Christian Writers Conferences

Writers conferences provide authors an excellent opportunity to meet and connect with other Christian authors as well as to stay abreast of the industry trends. More Christian writers conferences take place across the United States each year than can be mentioned here. An online search for "Christian writers conferences" will bring up a good list for you to peruse.

Join Online Author Discussion Groups

Another good way to get connected, network, and learn from others is to join online discussion groups for Christian authors. Joining discussion groups is free and it is a good avenue for acquiring encouragement and information. A sampling of online discussion groups for Christian authors is offered here.

- **ChristianWriters.com (CW)**
  The CW community includes a number of forums or discussion boards and a chat room for Christian authors. This group requires membership, but membership is free and easy to obtain online.
  www.christianwriters.com

- **Christian Writers Group International, Inc. (CWGI)**
  CWG offers an online discussion group as well as a message board for Christian writers.
  www.christianwritersgroup.org

- **FaithWriters.com**
  FaithWriters requires membership, but membership is free and easy to obtain online. This community provides message boards and discussion forums as well as other opportunities for writers to network and grow.
  www.faithwriters.com

- **Christian Electronic Authors**
  Owned by Christian e-Author, this group discusses electronic publishing and inspirational writing for electronic books. They investigate inspirational writing, promotional opportunities for electronic books, e-publishers, and the world of electronic publishing.
  http://groups.yahoo.com/group/Christian-e-author

Summary

C.S. Lewis once said, "The next best thing to being wise oneself is to live in a circle of those who are." Being a member of an association or discussion group places you in a circle of wise people. Associating with and learning from other people in your field helps you become wiser in your own business.

Gather Endorsements

*For it is not the one who commends himself who is approved,
but the one whom the Lord commends.*
—2 Corinthians 10:18

> Marketing Fundamental:
> **A celebrity name sells books.**

Endorsements sell books. A good endorsement can make the difference between a few sales and a multitude of sales, especially for unknown and lesser-known authors. Publishers know this. That is why so many Christian personalities and celebrities are asked to endorse books of lesser-known authors.

Famous names sell books. That is why the name of the celebrity endorsing the book is placed prominently on the cover; often in larger font than the author's name and sometimes in larger font than the title. Acquiring endorsements is especially important in the Christian marketplace.

The Benefits of Endorsements

Why spend your time seeking endorsements for a book? Endorsements lend credibility to a book and state that the book has quality.

Endorsements Lend Credibility to a Book

The Christian marketplace is a harder market for an unknown author and publisher to break into than the secular marketplace. The main issue is credibility. How does a Christian book buyer receive assurances that a book is doctrinally sound? Christian consumers want assurance that a book will truly have a Christian message before purchasing. With so many books to choose from, most book buyers depend on name recognition; either the publisher's reputation or the author's reputation.

A good endorsement can make the difference between a few sales and a multitude of sales.

A new publisher or author often has no reputation and thus no credibility. Hence, an endorsement from a known Christian personality provides the credibility book buyers need to be assured that a book is doctrinally sound and appropriate for the Christian audience.

The more famous the person providing an endorsement is, the greater the influence will be on the potential book buyer.

However, any endorsement is better than no endorsements. Even a testimonial by a relatively unknown Christian person can be helpful in increasing the credibility of a book, especially if the person is linked to a Christian church or service organization that can be mentioned by name.

Endorsements State a Book Has Quality

Christian booksellers have limited shelf space from which to sell books. Distributors can only market a finite number of books and generally choose to represent those books they think have the greatest possibility of selling. Consumers have limited spending dollars and limited time to spend reading. Each of these important players in making book sales happen want to be assured that the book they will be purchasing is a quality book.

Endorsements, especially those by known Christian celebrities, give book buyers the message that the book set before them is a quality product worthy of their time, money, and shelf space.

Sarah Bolme

Securing Endorsements

Endorsements should be secured for a book while the book is still in manuscript form, long before it goes to print. When requesting an endorsement, make sure you send a copy of your manuscript for the endorser to review. It is acceptable to provide endorsers with a list of names of other persons from whom you are requesting endorsements. Most celebrity endorsers will be pleased to be included in good company and those who are not celebrities will be excited to have their names printed with famous people.

It is best to have endorsements secured prior to the galleys of the book being mailed out to secure book reviews (see chapter 5). That way, any endorsements can be listed on the galley and will help send the message to the potential reviewers that the book is worthy of their time.

Use of Endorsements

The name of a prominent endorser can be used on the front cover of a book if that person writes an introduction or foreword for the book. Positive statements made by endorsers should be included on the back cover of a book. Keep the statements short and powerful. The whole endorsement does not need to be printed, just the salient points. Additionally, endorsements should be listed on the book's website and all of the book's promotional materials.

Summary

For unknown authors and publishers seeking to break into the Christian market, endorsements are essential. Endorsements send the message that a book has a trustworthy Christian message and is worthy of the time and money a book buyer would invest in it.

3

Secure Distribution

Of making many books there is no end.
—Ecclesiastes 12:12

> Marketing Fundamental:
> **The more channels through which consumers can purchase your books, the more books you will sell.**

Distribution is key to reaching the Christian retail marketplace. Even with name recognition, endorsements, favorable Christian reviews, an ambitious marketing campaign, and a book award, without adequate distribution to the Christian retail market, a book will remain in your warehouse or at a POD printer.

In 2012, for the first time, more books (44%) were purchased online than were purchased in all types of brick-and-mortar stores (32%) including large retail chains, independent bookstores, other mass merchandisers, and supermarkets. Some authors and new publishers feel that distribution is not important because they are going to sell their books over the Internet and bypass stores. However, distribution is still important for ease of ordering. This chapter will focus on distribution for print books (see chapter 16 for distribution of ebook titles).

Just as a book must be easily accessible to retailers through established distribution channels to ensure retail orders, it must also be readily accessible in various locations (online or in stores) for consumers to purchase it. When a book is not readily available through the established distribution channels, retailers and consumers are less likely to pursue purchasing the title. The momentum you build through a fantastic marketing plan can easily be lost when your book is not readily available in the usual retail channels.

Not everyone buys from Amazon. Your book must be available in a variety of ways to ensure that your interested readers are able to purchase it easily in the fashion they like to purchase books. Some readers prefer to purchase books from their local bookstore. For these readers, your book must be available for them to order from a bookstore if it is not already stocked on the shelves. In order for retailers to be able to order your book, it must be in an established distribution channel.

Establish your distribution channel prior to the publication of your book.

Most Christian retailers prefer to order their products from a handful of sources. The fewer accounts they have to maintain, the easier their bookkeeping. A number of smaller orders to individual publishers generally results in more overhead and shipping costs for a store, which decreases the store's profit margin.

Establish your distribution channel prior to the publication of your book. When submitting your title for trade announcements and book reviews, it is important to let the book industry know that your book will be available for retail orders through readily accepted channels in the marketplace. Having distribution also helps secure reviewers' confidence in your product and increases the likelihood that your book will be evaluated for review.

Types of Distribution

Two main choices exist for making your book readily available to the Christian retail marketplace: wholesale book companies and distributors.

Wholesale Book Companies

Wholesale book companies purchase books from publishing companies and fulfill book orders from retail stores. Wholesale companies generally purchase books outright from a publisher, but debit the publisher's account when retailers return unsold books. These companies generally purchase books from a publisher at a 55 to 60 percent discount off the retail price. Some wholesale companies require the publisher to pay the shipping for books sold to their company. The wholesale company then sells the books to retail stores and libraries at a 40 to 45 percent discount.

Wholesale book companies provide no sales representation for the books they offer to retail outlets. All sales and marketing representation is the responsibility of the publishing company. Publishers must direct retail buyers to the wholesale company for ease of purchase. Wholesale companies offer publishers opportunities to advertise in their catalogs and other promotional materials that they send to bookstores and libraries on a regular basis.

Wholesale companies generally want to know the specifics of a publisher's marketing plans, advertising budget, and sales representation for titles prior to agreeing to purchase and stock a new publisher's titles.

Distributors

Distributors purchase books from publishing companies and sell these books to wholesalers, retail stores, and libraries. They provide sales representation (mostly to the larger and major chain bookstores) to promote the titles they sell. Most distributors purchase books from a publisher at a 65 to 70 percent discount off the retail price and most even have the publisher pay for shipping the books to the distributor. The distributor then sells the books to retailers at a 40 to 45 percent discount.

Distributors usually work on a consignment basis, only paying publishers for books they have sold. Most require publishers to pay storage costs for the books they hold in their warehouse. Distributors make the books they sell available for purchase through the major wholesale book companies to ensure more retail orders.

Generally, distributors operate under exclusive contracts, meaning that they handle all sales to the retail marketplace (publishers cannot sell directly to retail outlets, including online retailers). Although distributors provide some sales representation, they still expect publishers to continue to finance and run marketing campaigns for the books.

Christian Wholesale Book Companies

Currently there are three major wholesale book companies that focus directly on the Christian retail market. Almost all Christian bookstores have an account with one or more of these wholesalers and purchase books from them on a regular basis.

It is difficult for a new, emerging publisher in the Christian marketplace to secure an account with one of the three major Christian wholesale book companies. Spring Arbor requires that a publisher have a minimum of ten titles in print; the other two companies are more likely to accept a new publisher if that publishing company is advertising in one of the Christian retail marketing groups' promotional catalogs (see chapter 8), is publishing books by a known Christian personality, or has an exceptionally ambitious marketing campaign.

- **Anchor**
  A sister company of Whitaker House, Anchor is the smallest of the three Christian wholesale book companies.
  Anchor
  1030 Hunt Valley Circle
  New Kensington, PA 15068
  800-444-4484
  purchasing@anchordistributors.com
  www.anchordistributors.com

- **Send The Light, Inc. (STL)**
  Send The Light is a wholesale distributor of Christian materials, but also has a distribution division for smaller publishers.
  Sent The Light
  100 Biblica Way
  Elizabethton, TN 37643
  800-289-2772
  www.stl-distribution.com

- **Spring Arbor Distributors, Inc.**
  Spring Arbor is the largest of the wholesale companies. It is Ingram's Christian division. A publisher must have a minimum of 10 titles in print for Spring Arbor to consider purchasing and stocking titles. Publishers with less than 10 titles are encouraged to contract with

a distributor to have their titles made available through Spring Arbor. When a title is accepted by Spring Arbor, it is also available for retailers and librarians to order through Ingram's general market book channel.

bookbuyer@ingramcontent.com
www.springarbor.com

General Market Wholesale Book Companies

Publishers who wish to make their titles available for order by secular bookstores and librarians should also stock their titles with a general market wholesale book company. There are a number of wholesale book companies for the general market. The two largest are mentioned here.

- **Baker & Taylor, Inc.**
  Baker & Taylor sells books to the general retail market and the general library market. Baker & Taylor will accept small publishers' titles; however, there is a fee to join Baker & Taylor as a publisher supplier.

  For most small publishers, Baker & Taylor will list their titles as available for purchase by retailers and librarians, but they will not actually purchase the title from the publisher until a retail store or library places an order for the title. This can add up to larger shipping costs for small publishers when book orders from Baker & Taylor trickle in one or two books at a time.

  Baker & Taylor requires that new publishers submit an application. When the company receives an application, they contact the publisher with additional information. The application to become a publisher supplier with Baker & Taylor can be found on their website.

  www.btol.com/supplier_book_publishers.cfm

- **Ingram**
  Ingram sells books to the general retail market and the general library market. A publisher must have a minimum of 10 titles in print for Ingram to consider purchasing and stocking titles.

  bookbuyer@ingramcontent.com
  www.ingramcontent.com

Christian Marketplace Distributors

Many large Christian publishing houses have distribution departments that provide sales representation and order fulfillment for Christian retail stores and churches. Some large Christian publishing houses distribute for other Christian publishers who choose not to conduct their own sales and order fulfillment. There are a few distributors in the Christian marketplace who provide sales representation and order fulfillment for large and medium size Christian publishing houses.

These distributors include:

- **Wesscott Marketing, Inc.**
  www.wesscottmarketing.com

- **CNI Distribution**
  www.cnidist.com

- **Genesis Marketing Group's Revelation Marketing**
  www.revelationlink.com

Currently, there are four distributors for the Christian marketplace that work with small and self-publishers. Each sells the titles they carry to the major wholesale book companies and provides some type of sales presentation to Christian chain bookstores as well as at some Christian trade shows.

- **AtlasBooks Distribution Service**
  AtlasBooks is a division of BookMasters, Inc., a book printing and marketing company.
  AtlasBooks Distribution Service
  2541 Ashland Rd.
  PO Box 2139
  Mansfield, OH 44905
  800-537-6727
  info@atlasbooks.com
  www.atlasbooks.com

- **Catholic Word Publisher Group**
  Catholic Word partners with publishers of Catholic materials to provide distribution to Catholic bookstores and the Catholic market.
  Catholic Word Publisher Group
  W5180 Jefferson St.
  Necedah, WI 54646
  or
  2401 Harnish Dr., Ste. 100
  Algonquin, IL 60102
  800-932-3826
  Michele Sylvestro, Director of Sales
  msylvestro@catholicword.com
  www.catholicword.com

- **Advocate Distribution Solutions**
  Advocate Distribution Solutions is a division of wholesaler Send The Light (STL). They tend to work with mid-sized publishers, but will give consideration to small publishers.
  Advocate Distribution Solutions
  100 Biblica Way
  Elizabethton, TN 37643
  800-289-2772
  Darren Henry, VP of Advocate Distribution Solutions
  darren.henry@stl-distribution.com
  www.advocatedistribution.com

- **New Day Christian Distribution**
  Historically, this company has specialized in music, but it has now broadened its focus to gifts, books, and DVDs.
  New Day Christian Distributors
  126 Shivel Dr.
  Hendersonville, TN 37075
  800-251-3633
  www.newdaychristian.com

Additional Resource

Christian Small Publishers Association (CSPA) recognizes the difficulty that many new and small publishers have securing distribution. To help small publishers, this association offers its member publishers access to a distribution programs for listing and stocking titles with both Spring Arbor and Send The Light (STL).

- **Christian Small Publishers Association**
  Distribution is one of many services and benefits provided by this organization.
  CSPA
  PO Box 481022
  Charlotte, NC 28269
  704-277-7194
  cspa@christianpublishers.net
  www.christianpublishers.net

Distribution for Print-on-Demand Titles

With the advent of print-on-demand (POD), many smaller publishers and independently published authors no longer use offset printing and carry inventory on their books. Instead, it is much more cost-effective to have the books printed as they are sold. Fortunately, many POD companies offer distribution options along with printing and sales fulfillment of books.

> Fortunately, many POD companies offer distribution options.

Those authors and publishers who opt to use the distribution service through a POD company have fulfilled the requirements for national distribution since most POD companies stock the book in Ingram, making it available to both online and brick-and-mortar stores. A few POD companies offering this type of distribution include:

- **CreateSpace**
  CreateSpace has an expanded distribution option that lets authors distribute their title beyond Amazon.com.
  www.createspace.com

- **Lightning Source**
  Lightning Source offers distribution to the trade channel via Ingram for a small fee of $12 per year per title. Authors and publishers can also request that Lightning Source review the book for placement in Ingram's Christian division, Spring Arbor.
  www.lightningsource.com

- **Ingram Spark**
  This program of Ingram offers trade distribution for an annual fee of $12 per year per title.
  www.ingramspark.com

- **Snowfall Press**
  Snowfall Press has a retail distribution agreement via Send The Light, Inc., that authors and publishers can sign up for. This agreement carries an initial title listing fee and also has some ongoing distribution fees when books are sold. However, it does ensure that your books are available in the Christian trade channel.
  www.snowfallpress.com

When distribution for a book is secured through a distributor or a POD company, not only is the book available for brick-and-mortar bookstores to purchase, the book is also made available for consumers to order via online bookstores. If you choose to not secure distribution, then you will have to apply directly with each online bookstore (e.g., Amazon.com or BarnesAndNoble.com) to have your books placed in that particular online store. Some online bookstores charge a fee to set up an account with an independently published author or small publisher.

Summary

One of the biggest mistakes new small or self-publishers make is to neglect the distribution aspect of their marketing plan. Securing distribution sends a signal to the book trade industry that you are serious about marketing your books. Having national distribution through a distributor or wholesale book company selling books to the Christian marketplace is vital for securing book reviews and book orders from the Christian marketplace.

4

Announce Your Books

*Give praise to the Lord, proclaim his name;
make known among the nations
what he has done.*
—1 Chronicles 16:8

> Marketing Fundamental:
> **Never pass up an opportunity for free publicity.**

Announcing a new book is a way to get the public interested in your upcoming title even before it hits the street. Publishers have a small window of opportunity to announce and promote new titles to the book industry (retailers, librarians, and book reviewers).

The book industry is always looking for the next new book. Announcements of new titles catch both the industry's and the public's attention and generate much more interest than titles that have been around for awhile.

Trade Announcements

Trade announcements let you unveil your title to the marketplace prior to publication, alerting retailers, librarians, media personnel, and book reviewers of your upcoming title. Generally, you should make your trade announcements three to six months prior to the release of your title. Take advantage of the opportunities in the Christian marketplace for announcing an upcoming title since these announcements are usually free and a prudent marketing strategy.

> Make your trade announcements three to six months prior to release.

Christian Books Database

When you assign an ISBN to a book, Bowker, the ISBN agency, requests that you register your ISBN and the title of the book so that they can include the book in their Books in Print® database. Bowker's Books in Print database strives to be a comprehensive listing of all books containing ISBNs in the marketplace.

The Christian marketplace has its own version of Bowker's Books in Print for Christian titles.

- **Christian Books & More Database**

  This database is to the Christian retail market what Bowker's Books in Print is to the general booksellers market. Christian Books & More strives to provide a complete list of all Christian products for sale to the Christian retail market. It is free to list products in the Christian Books & More Database.

  The Christian Books & More Database is used by over 1,200 Christian stores for ordering and tracking product. It is also used to power some of the online Christian bookstore search engines such as Parable.com®.

  If you are marketing a book to the Christian retail marketplace, it is essential to get it listed in Christian Books & More Database. Listing is free, and instructions for submitting titles are available on their website.

  800-997-6724
  support@bsmgr.com
  www.bookstoremanager.com/vendor/cbm.aspx

Christian Retail Magazines

Currently, there are two magazines designed for Christian retailers, and both include coverage of upcoming titles in addition to product reviews. Name recognition is just as important for the editors of these Christian retail magazines as it is for Christian retailers. Therefore, when submitting a press release about your upcoming title, if your book is not by a known Christian personality, make sure that you include your membership in a Christian publishers association, your distribution for the Christian retail market, any celebrity endorsements, and other pertinent data providing assurance of a quality Christian product.

- **CBA Retailers + Resources**
  This magazine is produced by CBA, The Association for Christian Retail. A subscription to *CBA Retailers + Resources* is included with a retailer's CBA membership.

  Send announcements regarding your new products releases to info@cbaonline.org.
  www.cbaonline.org

- **Christian Retailing**
  Produced by Charisma Media, this publication is geared toward Christian retailers. The magazine is free to any bookstore actively selling Christian products in the United States.

  Send press releases for editorial review and inclusion in *Christian Retailing* to Chris Johnson, General Editor, who can be reached at chris.johnson@charismamedia.com.

  You can also submit new releases for free for Christian retailers to see directly on *Christian Retailing*'s website under the "New Products" tab.
  www.christianretailing.com

Other Trade Announcements

Some general market publications offer free upcoming title announcements. Take advantage of these free listings for your titles. While these publications are not strictly for the Christian marketplace, many Christian retailers keep abreast of the larger book industry as well as the Christian industry and thus subscribe to these publications. Since many general market bookstores and libraries carry religious titles and exposure is an essential element in a book's success, submitting your title to these listings is sensible marketing.

— Sarah Bolme —

- **Publishers Weekly**
  PW is the top trade journal of the publishing industry. Used widely by publishers, book reviewers, retailers, and librarians, it is produced on a weekly basis and covers all the current news for the publishing industry. *Publishers Weekly* features spring and fall book announcements for adult books, children's books, and religious books.

  PW's Religious Book Announcements include religion/spirituality/ inspirational and children's religious books. Marcia Z. Nelson is the religion editor for *PW*. She edits the biannual Religion Announcements. Contact her at mnelson@publishersweekly.com to request to be placed on the mailing list to receive submission notices for the spring and fall Religion Announcements.

  www.publishersweekly.com

- **Library Journal**
  This journal is an adult book review publication for public and academic librarians. It features upcoming title announcements for spring and fall in two issues during the year. Their editorial calendar on their website provides information on which issues the announcements appear in and submission deadlines.

  For information on how to submit a title for announcement, contact Margaret Heilbrun at mheilbrun@mediasourceinc.com

  www.libraryjournal.com

- **Booklist**
  This monthly publication of the American Library Association provides reviews of books for librarians across the country. It also features seasonal book announcements for new titles.

  Title announcements should be addressed to Brad Hooper at bhooper@ala.org for adult books, or to Gillian Engberg at gengberg@ala.org for young adult and children's books.

  www.ala.org/booklist

- **Small Press Record of Books in Print**
  Produced annually by Dustbooks, this record is a listing of books in print by small and self-publishers. Title submissions can be made online on their website.

  www.dustbooks.com

- *Foreword Reviews*
  This quarterly publication aimed largely at librarians, does not provide a listing of upcoming titles. However, each issue features a ForeSight section that covers current trends or perspectives in various book genres. You can find the editorial calendar listing the categories each issue will cover on the *Foreword Reviews* website. The magazine considers new books to feature in their ForeSight section three months in advance of the publication date. Send your upcoming or new title for review to:
  Foreword Reviews / ForeSight
  425 Boardman Ave. Suite B
  Traverse City, MI 49684
  www.forewordreviews.com

- *BookPage*
  This monthly publication aimed at booksellers and librarians also does not provide a listing of upcoming titles. However, in addition to providing reviews of books, each issue of the journal highlights books of seasonal interest. The editorial calendar for these subjects can be found on *BookPage*'s website. To submit a new or upcoming book for review consideration in one of the seasonal features, send a galley or finished copy of the book three months prior to the relevant issue date to:
  BookPage
  attn: Lynn Green, Editor
  2143 Belcourt Ave.
  Nashville, TN 37212
  www.bookpage.com

General Announcements

Announcing a book to generate interest and buzz about your upcoming title is an important part of a marketing plan. In addition to announcing your book to the book trade for retailers, librarians, and other book buyers to discover, announce your book to your target audience.

Bookstores & Libraries

Many secular bookstores and public libraries carry Christian titles. Announcing your new book to book buyers in libraries and secular bookstores can bring additional sales. Below are two services to help you get the word out to these buyers.

- **Publishers Portal**
  Publishers Portal is a service that helps publishers and authors place their book excerpts in front of millions of book buyers, book dealers, and librarians. This company creates and distributes first chapter book excerpts to major ecommerce book sellers, book distributors, and librarians.

  Publishers Portal places first chapter excerpts on databases maintained by Ingram and Baker & Taylor, as well as databases used by libraries such as those supplied by Content Café and Bowker Books in Print. They also make the first chapter excerpt available on BarnesAndNoble.com for any book available on that website.

  Publishers Portal's service is for any book containing an ISBN. Best of all, it is very affordable. The cost to have Publishers Portal place first chapter book excerpts of your book in databases around the Internet is just $30.00.

  info@publishersportal.com
  www.publishersportal.com

- **ABA's Advanced Access Program**
  Each month the American Booksellers Association's Advanced Access program emails over 1,000 independent booksellers with news of galleys, reading copies, or finished books that publishers are offering for review. After receiving a free review copy from you, stores will read and decide whether to carry the title. The Advance Access program makes no promises, but has proved to be a very effective way to get the word out about titles. Stores email you directly, and generally, you can expect requests from 25 to 50 booksellers.

  The cost to participate in Advanced Access is $150; contact Pete Reynolds at peter@bookweb.org or 914-406-7535.

  www.bookweb.org

Professional Associations

When announcing your book, you shouldn't overlook the various professional associations, including publishers or writers associations, of which you are a member. Send your new book announcements to these organizations as most publishers and writers associations include new book announcements in the newsletter or journal they produce for their members.

Social Networking

Build buzz around an upcoming title by letting your followers on your social networking sites know that status of your upcoming book and when to expect it to be available to purchase (for more on social networking, see chapter 14). You can also include an announcement on your various discussion groups. Many discussion groups allow you to post new book announcements.

Previous Customers

If you have a mailing list of customers who have previously purchased books from you or your publishing company, use this list to generate a pre-publication announcement for your new titles. Whether you mail a postcard, letter, or brochure, or send an email announcement, make sure to include ordering information in your notice. New book announcements sent via email or snail mail to your established customers will result in more orders for your new titles.

Summary

Many authors and small publishers don't think about marketing until they have their books in hand. Announcing your book in the months leading up to your publication date can help jump-start your sales.

5

Garner Book Reviews

Let another praise you, and not your own mouth;
someone else, and not your own lips.
—Proverbs 27:2

> Marketing Fundamental:
> **Book reviews open doors for book sales.**

Book reviews are an essential element of any book launch and marketing campaign. Reviews generate the interest of book buyers and provide publishers with a great low-cost marketing tool. For the cost of a book and postage, a review can supply praise and exposure for your books.

Favorable reviews by reputable review sources provide your book recognition in the Christian marketplace. Reviews also bring broader exposure for your titles. Every publication providing reviews of books has a readership base awaiting those reviews. A review in a publication geared toward the Christian marketplace exposes all of its readers to your title. Even an unfavorable review still provides exposure. In fact, sometimes unfavorable reviews actually drive more people to buy a book, especially if the opinion of the reviewer sparks controversy or disagreement.

A complimentary review by a reputable review source is gold to a publisher. Every review a book secures can and should be used repeatedly in your marketing campaign. Favorable reviews (or excerpts from them) should be posted on your website, printed on all your marketing materials, used in advertisements, and added to your book's cover on subsequent print runs.

Reviews of books break down into two categories: trade reviews and reviews for consumers. Trade reviews are reviews geared toward the retail marketplace. These reviews alert retailers and librarians of upcoming books and provide a short synopsis of the book with an opinion (by the reviewer) as to how the book will be received by consumers. Reviews for consumers are similar to industry trade reviews except that they are geared to book buyers and readers. Consumer reviews also provide a short synopsis of the book and an opinion (by the reviewer) on whether the book is worth investing the time to read it.

Materials to Include When Requesting a Review

Presentation is important in every aspect of marketing books, including submissions for review. The following items are the essential elements for a book review request package.

A Cover Letter

The information you provide in the cover letter should include the title of the book, the author, the book's category, the publisher, the ISBN, book binding (e.g., paperback, hardcover), retail price, number of illustrations and page count, the publication date, any distributors, and your overall marketing plan for the book. Having both distribution and a strong marketing plan boosts your chances of being reviewed. Publications prefer to review books that they feel will sell well, and the stronger the marketing plan, the greater the chances a book will sell (and, therefore, that it will get a review).

A Fact Sheet or a Press Release

A fact sheet or press release should summarize how your book is distinctive and different from other books. It should also contain the exact title of the book, the author's name, publication date, ISBN, retail price, contact information for the publisher of the book, and ordering information. Including a section on the author's credentials for writing the book and including the names of other books by the author adds credence to your book. Outlines and samples of press releases can be found online at PRWeb Press Release Newswire (www.prweb.com/pressreleasetips.php) and Publicity Insider (www.publicityinsider.com/release.asp).

The Actual Book or Galley

Most review publications specify whether they want one or two copies of either the galley or the actual book to review. Those requesting galleys require that they be sent three to six months in advance of publication (the date your book becomes available for sale), while those desiring the actual book to review expect to get the book within the first few months of the publication date. A galley (also called an Advance Reading Copy or ARC) is typically a print-on-demand version of the book with either a generic cover containing the important facts or the actual cover stating the book is an Advanced Reading Copy. Some publications now accept digital galleys. Be sure to check whether a reviewer is willing to accept a digital galley before submitting one via email.

Christian Trade Reviews

When submitting a galley for review by a Christian trade review source, send a query to the reviewer describing your book prior to sending the actual galley. Make sure you include all information necessary to secure the reviewer's confidence that you have a reputable Christian product.

Information in a query should include any endorsements by known Christian personalities, any Christian publishers association memberships, a thumbnail sketch of your marketing plans, and who will be distributing the book to the Christian marketplace. The reviewer will then let you know if they are interested in reviewing your book, saving you time as well as possible wasted materials and postage.

- **CBA Retailers + Resources**

  This publication reviews galleys at least three months prior to publication. Query the editor at info@cbaonline.org.

  CBA Retailers + Resources
  9240 Explorer Drive, Suite 200
  Colorado Springs, CO 80920
  719-272-3510
  www.cbaonline.org

- **Christian Retailing**
  This magazine reviews galleys at least three months prior to the date of publication. Prior to submitting, query the Editor, Chris D. Johnson at chris.johnson@charismamedia.com.
  Christian Retailing
  600 Rinehart Rd.
  Lake Mary, FL 32746
  407-333-0600
  www.christianretailing.com

General Trade Reviews

The following trade review sources include reviews of religious titles in their publications. While these trade reviews are geared toward the general book market, they are reputable review sources and recognized as such by Christian retailers. It is always wise to query the reviewer for these publications prior to mailing your books for review.

Most of these publications have their submission criteria on their webpage. Some do not want publishers to contact them prior to submitting a book for review. These publications receive so many books to review that they prefer less communication. Some provide a contact to use after your submission is sent and others request that you do not contact them after submission; they will contact you if your book is chosen for review.

Some review publications request that you submit more than one copy of your title in galley or book form. The publications that request galleys usually also request that you submit copies of the actual book when it becomes available. This is really only necessary for those publications that are providing a review of your title.

Since book reviews are a low-cost marketing effort, submitting titles for review is always a prudent marketing tactic (even to the larger review publications) as you never know when your book may be chosen for a review.

> Even an unfavorable review still provides exposure.

- **Booklist**
  This publication of the American Library Association provides reviews of books for librarians across the country. Submit galleys for adult books to Brad Hooper, Adult Books Editor, at bhooper@ala.org; and for young adult and children's books to Gillian Engberg, Books for Youth Editor, at gengberg@ala.org.
  Booklist
  American Library Association
  50 E Huron
  Chicago, IL 60611
  www.ala.org/booklist

- **BookPage**
  BookPage: America's Book Review provides reviews of books for booksellers and librarians. This publication reviews all types of books except for poetry, print-on-demand, and self-published titles. Submit galleys at least three months prior to publication, flagged to the attention of the appropriate editor as listed on their website.
  BookPage
  2143 Belcourt Ave.
  Nashville, TN 37212
  www.bookpage.com

- **ForeWord Reviews**
  This bimonthly pre-publication review journal has a circulation of around 8,000 booksellers, librarians, and industry professionals with a readership of 16,000. The magazine provides reviews of books published by small and independent publishing houses. *ForeWord Magazine* matches their print review with the month of the publication date of the title, so they only accept galleys three to four months in advance of publication date.
  Digital galleys can be submitted to aimee@forewordreviews.com.
  ForeWord Reviews
  attn: Book Review Editor
  425 Boardman Avenue
  Traverse City, Michigan 49684.
  www.forewordreviews.com

- **The Horn Book Magazine and The Horn Book Guide**
  These distinguished journals only review young adult and children's literature. *The Horn Book Magazine* is published bimonthly. *The Horn Book Guide* is published semi-annually. These publications require two copies of new titles to be sent for review to:
  The Horn Book, Inc.
  56 Roland Street, Suite 200
  Boston, MA 02129
  info@hbook.com
  www.hbook.com

- **Library Journal**
  This adult book review journal is for public and academic librarians. Their complete submission requirements are listed on the website. Submit galleys in advance of publication to:
  Library Journal
  Book Review Editor
  160 Varick St., 11th Floor
  New York, New York 10013
  www.libraryjournal.com

- **Midwest Book Review**
  The Midwest Book Review is an organization committed to promoting literacy, library usage, and small press publishing. They give consideration to small press publishers, self-published authors, academic presses, and specialty publishers. Several monthly publications are published by the Midwest Book Review for community and academic library systems.

  The Midwest Book Review only accepts books that are already in print and available to the public. Only published copies (no galleys or uncorrected proofs) are accepted for review. Submissions for review should be directed to:
  Midwest Book Review
  attn: James A. Cox, Editor-in-Chief
  278 Orchard Drive
  Oregon, WI 53575
  www.midwestbookreview.com

- *Publishers Weekly*
    This is the preeminent trade journal of the publishing industry. Used widely by publishers, book reviewers, booksellers, and librarians, it is produced on a weekly basis and features reviews of new books. Instructions on what to send with your galley are listed on the *Publishers Weekly* website under "Submission Guidelines." Submission for Christian book reviews should be directed to:
    Publishers Weekly
    attn: Marcia Z. Nelson
    Religion Reviews
    1118 Garfield St.
    Aurora, IL 60506
    mnelson@publishersweekly.com
    www.publishersweekly.com

    Publishers Weekly also offers reviews for self-published books in their special PW Select monthly section dedicated to covering the self-publishing industry. This section features interviews with authors, book announcements and listings, news, features, analysis, and book reviews. They charge a $149 fee to review a self-published book. Submission information is on the website.
    www.publishersweekly.com/pw/diy/index.html

Reviews for Church Librarians

Large numbers of churches across the United States host a church library in their building for their members' reading enrichment. Church library associations exist to provide services and resources for these libraries. One of these services is the production of a newsletter or journal to encourage and educate church librarians. These publications all contain reviews of new books that might be of interest to the church libraries they reach.

Church library publications review books that are new (within a few months of publication date) rather than galleys. As with any book review request, it is wise to query editors with information about your book to make sure that your title fits with each publication's audience prior to submitting your book for review.

- *Catholic Library World*
  This is a publication of The Catholic Library Association that is published quarterly. Submit books for review to:
  CLA
  100 North Street, Suite 224
  Pittsfield, MA 01201-5109
  www.cathla.org

- *Church Libraries*
  This is published quarterly by the Evangelical Church Library Association, a national organization for church and Christian school librarians. Materials for review must be published in the past year and be conservative, evangelical, and non-charismatic. *Church Libraries* does not review self-published books, ebooks, or print-on-demand books.
  Church Libraries
  attn: Lin Johnson, Managing Editor
  9118 W Elmwood Dr. #1G
  Niles, IL 60714-5820
  lin@eclalibraries.org.
  www.eclalibraries.org

- *Congregational Libraries Today*
  This is a quarterly publication of the Church and Synagogue Library Association, which serves congregational libraries of all faiths.
  Congregational Libraries Today
  attn: Monica Tenney, Book Review Editor
  399 Blenheim Rd.
  Columbus, OH 43214
  614-262-4625
  motenney@aol.com
  http://cslainfo.org

- *The Lamplighter*
  The Pacific Northwest Association of Church Libraries assists in the establishment and operation of church libraries in the Pacific Northwest states. It produces *The Lamplighter* quarterly for its members.
  For book reviews, query either June Ruyle, Book Review Editor, at junepnacl@juno.com; or Susan Reiver, Lamplighter Editor, at rprser@uswest.net.
  www.pnacl.org

- **The Christian Librarian**
  This journal is published three times a year by the Association of Christian Librarians, which serves evangelical librarians serving in institutes of higher learning, mostly Christian colleges and seminaries.
  Association of Christian Librarians
  attn: Phyllis Fox, Review Editor
  PO Box 4
  Cedarville, OH 45314
  pfox@pointloma.edu
  www.acl.org

Reviews for Christian Consumers

The two publications listed in this section review either galleys or newly published books for Christian readers. These publications are aimed at the general Christian marketplace and have large circulations.

Many more Christian magazines exist for specific markets (for more information on garnering reviews and coverage of your titles in Christian magazines, please refer to chapter 11).

As with trade reviews, whenever possible, query the book review editor first before submitting your book for review. Again, make sure you include all information necessary to secure the reviewer's confidence that you have a reputable Christian product readily available to readers in the marketplace.

- **Books & Culture: A Christian Review**
  Books & Culture is a bimonthly review of books produced by Christianity Today International. The editor of *Books & Culture* is also the editor-at-large for *Christianity Today* magazine.
  Christianity Today International
  attn: John Wilson, Editor
  465 Gundersen Dr.
  Carol Stream, IL 60188
  877-247-4787
  bceditor@booksandculture.com
  www.booksandculture.com

- **WORLD Magazine**
    This magazine provides weekly news from a Christian viewpoint. It is a Christian counterpart to general market news magazines like *Newsweek* and *Time*.

    Query Marvin Olasky at molasky@worldmag.com for youth and adult book reviews, and Susan Olasky at solasky@worldmag.com for children's book reviews.

    WORLD Magazine
    Box 20002
    Asheville, NC 28802
    www.worldmag.com

Online Christian Book Review Sites

There are many sites on the Internet dedicated to providing reviews of books. Most of these are traditional websites, but a few are blogs that are dedicated to book reviews. These sites provide many additional opportunities such as author interviews and advertisements to increase the exposure of your titles to Christian consumers, which generally amounts to more book sales. Most online Christian book review sites have a steady readership who frequent their site or at least receive the site's e-newsletter with information on the latest Christian titles for their reading pleasure.

Most sites publish their submission criteria or have a contact person listed for you to request the submission criteria.

General Christian Titles (both fiction and nonfiction)

- www.christianbookpreviews.com
- www.faithfulreader.com
- www.christianbookwormreviews.com
- www.readerviews.com
- http://thefriendlybooknook.com
- http://readersfavorite.com/book-reviews.htm
- http://christianbooknotes.com
- http://thechristianmanifesto.com
- http://radiantlit.com

Christian Fiction Titles

- www.christianfictionreview.com
- www.catholicfiction.net
- www.fictionaddict.com
- www.edgyinspirationalromance.com
- www.christianfictionbookreviews.org
- www.rtbookreviews.com/genre/inspirational
- www.familyfiction.com
- www.thesuspensezone.com

Christian Young Adult and Children's Titles

- www.ccbreview.blogspot.com
- www.ateenzfaith.com
- www.akidzfaith.com
- www.readerviewskids.com
- www.teenreads.com
- www.kidsreads.com
- www.clashentertainment.com
- www.20somethingreads.com
- http://graphicnovelreporter.com

Christian Science Fiction / Fantasy

- www.mindflights.com

Book Reviews for a Fee

There are plenty of ways to secure free book reviews. However, if you are desperate for a review, you can always pay to have a review of your book. The following book review sites review books for a fee. Fees range from $50 to over $200 per title.

- http://onlinereviewofbooks.com
- www.bookpleasures.com
- www.fearlessbooks.com/Reviews.html
- www.theusreview.com

Consumer Reviews

Reviews by readers are another important element in creating a positive climate to sell your books. While reader reviews may not generate as much exposure as dedicated review publications or websites, they are important for consumers when they are shopping for a book. Many readers check out the reviews posted on an online retail site before committing to purchase a book. One survey showed that 70% of consumers reported that online consumer reviews were the second most trusted source of information for purchasing decisions. Consumers want to know what other readers are saying about a book before investing time and money in it. A lack of reader reviews on retail sites such as Amazon.com and BarnesAndNoble.com has the potential to hinder sales.

> *70% of consumers reported that online consumer reviews were the second most trusted source of information.*

Readers

In addition to professional review venues, seek out a few readers to read your book in advance of publication with the agreement that they will send you a copy of their review and place it on a retail website. Find these reader reviewers by asking other writers in your writing groups, seeking out individuals in your church that match your target audience, or making a request on any online discussion groups where the readers might be interested in your book. You can also find reviewers via social networking. For example, the social reading networking site Goodreads (www.goodreads.com) offers a program for authors to give away free books to readers. The author chooses the number of books to give, and Goodreads picks the winners. Winners of the free books are not required, but are encouraged, to write reviews.

Bloggers

Getting bloggers to review your book is another way to spread the word about your book online. Blogs hold a lot of influential power on purchasing decisions of consumers. In fact, blogs ranked third (behind retail sites and brand sites) in impacting consumers' decision to purchase a product. Bloggers carry influence with their reading audiences. Therefore, if a blogger gives a book a favorable review, her audience is more likely to purchase the book.

You can approach bloggers that are writing to your target audience about the possibility of reviewing your book. Many bloggers provide reviews of books in exchange for a copy of the book. Christian Small Publishers Association (CSPA) has a program to help its members find bloggers to review their books. This program, BookCrash (www.bookcrash.com), gives free books to bloggers in exchange for a review of the book posted on their blog and one retail website.

Another service that helps publishers and authors find pre-publication reviews of their books is NetGalley.

- **NetGalley**
  NetGalley offers publishers the ability to find professional reviews for their galleys. With the NetGalley Marketing Program, publishers have the ability to share their advance reader galleys electronically and instantly (with full anti-copying protection applied) with 145,000+ reviewers, media, booksellers, librarians, and bloggers. Single titles can be set up with NetGalley for a listing fee of $399. This allows the title to be available for six months for professional readers to request to review.
  www.netgalley.com

After a Review

Jesus healed ten men with leprosy; only one remembered to return to thank him. Be like the one. When you receive a book review, remember to send a thank-you note to the reviewer.

Not only is it polite and thoughtful, it will ingratiate you with the reviewer so that when your next title is placed in front of him, he will be more likely to take the time to review it.

Summary

Reviews provide an independent opinion of your book for consumers to use when making a purchasing decision. Good book reviews lend credibility to your title. They let potential readers know that your book is worth the money and the time they will invest in it. Post excerpts from reviews on your website, use them in all your marketing and advertising materials, and include them in your book on the next print run.

Host a Book Launch Event

A scroll of remembrance was written in his presence concerning those who feared the LORD and honored his name.
—Malachi 3:16

> Marketing Fundamental:
> **Out-of-the-box, creative ideas are often the most effective marketing strategies.**

Producing a book is similar to the plot line in a novel. A fiction work has five parts to the plot line: exposition, rising action, climax, falling action, and resolution. In producing a book, creating the manuscript is the exposition. The rising action is all those things that must be done to make the manuscript ready for publication. This includes editing and proofing, cover design, interior layout, obtaining endorsements, securing distribution, and building up excitement for launch. The climax is when the book is finally published and becomes available for the general public to purchase. This is followed by the falling action, which is all the ongoing marketing efforts after publication to continue to sell the book. Lastly, resolution occurs when attention is turned to the next book and the process starts all over again.

The point at which a book becomes available for purchase is the climax of the publishing process. This event should not pass without some type of fanfare. Many authors plan some sort of book launch event to commemorate this occasion and to garner additional publicity and hype for a new book. In today's world, you have two main ways to host a book launch party: you can hold a physical event where people attend in person at a physical location, or you can hold a virtual party online where people participate via their computer or mobile device.

Physical Event

A physical book launch event can range from a private party at a home or restaurant for just the people who have been instrumental in bringing the book to fruition, to a large public event at a rented hall. If your goal is to use your book launch to gain more publicity, then you should host a public book launch event designed for that purpose. There are a few factors to consider when putting on a book launch event. These include location, type of event, entertainment, and promotion.

Location

Book launch events can be held in a wide variety of locales. You can hold one in your local bookstore. This type of event is a nice partnership benefiting both the author and the store. Bookstores tend to embrace this type of event because it brings in customers. If you are promoting your event, then you are bringing business to the bookstore. Book launch events can also be held in a restaurant, a church, a local park, or a rented hall. Often, the type of event you choose to hold will determine where you host the event.

Type of Event

Your book launch event can range from a simple book signing, to an event that includes a reading, lecture, or discussion, to a full-fledged party including refreshments and music. Remember, the more party-like the event, the more people are likely to attend. Consider a theme for your book launch event that ties into the content of your book. For example, if your book has to do with Christmas, make Christmas the theme of your event.

One way to gather more publicity and a larger crowd for your event is to partner with another entity. Some authors have partnered with a local band so that their party had live music. This type of partnership provides publicity for the local band as well as the author. Both the book and the band's CDs can be offered for sale at the event. Others have partnered with a local nonprofit organization. If you are giving part of the proceeds from your book to a charity, make it a charity that you can invite to be present at your book launch party. This way you get more publicity and the charity gets more exposure. Partnering with either a business or an organization is a great way to increase the reach of your book launch party and thus increase your exposure.

Entertainment

What makes a good party? Most people would agree that people, stimulating conversation or activities, and refreshments are the most important elements for a great party. Therefore, make sure that you have some *The completion of your book should not pass without some type of fanfare.* form of entertainment at your book launch event. This does not need to be music or dancers. Your entertainment can be refreshments and door prizes. Make sure that you have some nice refreshments to serve to those who come to your party (if they are allowed in your venue). A cake and drinks are not that expensive and can make your event more appealing. Also, don't forget the door prizes. Give away a few copies of your book (or previous books) during your event. Hold a drawing or competition for the free copies. If you have partnered with another entity then make sure you have some prizes from that organization to give away. For example, if you have a book on beauty and have partnered with a local Avon® representative, then give away Avon product samples as part of your event.

Promotion

A public book launch party is just like a private affair in that you have to invite people to get attendees. Remember to begin inviting people plenty of time in advance. Give at least a month's notice and continue to remind people as the event draws nearer. In addition to your family and friends, you want to invite the general public, specifically those to whom your book is targeted. To invite this group of people, you can do the following:

- Write a press release announcing your event and send it to local media.
- Send an announcement to all the local events calendars in your area such as the local newspaper, your local church, the events section on Craigslist, and any other websites or publications that target your specific audience and promote local events.

- Send an announcement to your email list.
- Promote your event on social media: Facebook, Twitter, LinkedIn, Pinterest, etc.
- If you are hosting the event in a local bookstore, ask the manager if you can create flyers to put in the store's bags to notify their customers of the upcoming event.
- Make a poster advertising the event and hang it up at local businesses that allow it.
- Create a sign to be used on the day of the event at the location so people know they have come to the right place. This puts attendees at ease right from the start.
- Be sure to invite the media to attend. Any coverage you might get means you gather more publicity.

Creativity

The more creative you are, the more interesting your event is and the more attention it will draw. One author who wrote a book on martial arts hosted his book launch party at a martial arts center and provided martial arts demonstrations. This was a win for both the author and the martial arts center as it made more potential customers aware of their services. Be sure to have a photographer on hand (this can be a friend) to take pictures of the event. Use these pictures on your social networking sites to continue promoting your book.

Virtual Event

As the book market becomes more global, book fans become more widespread, stretching around the globe. As a result, virtual parties are increasing in popularity. Instead of hosting a book launch party at your local bookstore drawing a handful of people from only one area, you can host an event in the virtual world. Instead of renting a hall and throwing a physical party for a book launch, have your party online and expand your reach.

Virtual parties are similar to physical parties. They have all the same elements, so make sure you don't skip any of the important components like inviting people, having entertainment (lively conversation), and refreshments (in virtual parties, these are your giveaways).

Twitter Party

Twitter parties are live events held on Twitter. Twitter is a social media website where users type a 140 character (or less) phrase that goes out via a feed and shows up on pages as a stream of real-time items or "Tweets." A Twitter party is a way of connecting online at a virtual party of Tweets that are given a specific hashtag (for example #JohnsonParty), which allows everyone's Tweets to show up on the same page.

Twitter parties are usually an hour or two in length and have a certain topic or theme that draws people to them. They are free to attend; all the attendees need is a Twitter account. Party attendees become part of the fun by tweeting the specific hashtag in each message they send during the event. This hashtag is determined ahead of time by the author and provided to all invitees. Attendees enjoy Twitter parties because they are entertaining, informative, interactive, and can be attended from the comfort of their own home or office.

On Twitter, you can follow conversations in your Twitter feed, or by tracking a hashtag feed. Therefore, Twitter parties do not require that the people attending your party follow you on Twitter. As long as they use your party's hashtag, they will be part of the event.

Be sure to create buzz and invite people to your Twitter party. No one can attend if they don't know about it or plan for it. Also, just as with a physical party, a virtual party is about entertainment. Make sure your conversation is lively. Have a number of tweets planned ahead of time that are designed to engage people and generate discussion. Offer a few copies of your book for free to party attendees. Mail or email (if giving away digital copies) the book to attendees after the party.

For those that are intimidated by the thought of hosting a virtual Twitter party, there are services online that will help you do this, often for a fee. Two services to help you manage a Twitter party are #Twubs (www.twubs.com) and TweeParties (www.tweeparties.com).

Facebook Party

A Facebook party is similar to a physical party but held in the virtual world on your Facebook business page. The difference between a Twitter party and a Facebook party is that to attend your Facebook party, the attendee must be your fan on Facebook (that is, they must have "Liked" your page).

As with all parties, invite your fans to join you at a certain time on your Facebook page. During that time, party attendees will visit with you and your other party guests, ask questions, and interact with your company or organization and each other.

Following are some considerations when planning and hosting a Facebook book launch party:

- A Facebook party works best with pages that have at least 250 Facebook fans (more fans is always better).
- While some physical parties don't have an end time, it is important for a virtual party to have definite beginning and end times. The party can run anywhere from 1 hour to 6 hours. Remember that the author has to be present the entire time the party is in operation.
- When deciding the date and time of your party, keep in mind that your fans don't all live in your time zone. Be sure to choose a time that works well for a number of different time zones and a day that would work well for your fan base.
- Have a theme for your party. It can be a celebratory party or it can be a topic-oriented party to get your fans asking questions and talking about a specific topic.
- Don't forget to send out lots of invites. Facebook parties are not exclusive events, so make sure your fans know they can invite their friends to attend the party also.
- Be sure to offer goodies. Since a Facebook party is a virtual party, instead of food, have a lineup of free products to give away during the party; consider them door prizes.
- During the party make sure to converse with your guests, just like at a real party. Be polite and gracious.
- When the party is over, ensure that the winners get their prizes, and thank everyone for coming.

Summary

The climax of the publishing process is when a book has been brought to fruition. Don't pass up this opportunity both to celebrate the birth of your book and to generate publicity to increase sales for the book. Whether you hold a physical or a virtual launch party, an event will help you spread the word about your book.

Part Two

Selling Your Books

Pursue Book Awards

Do you see a man skilled in his work?
He will serve before kings; he will not serve before obscure men.
—Proverbs 22:29

> Marketing Fundamental:
> **Book awards influence buyers.**

Book awards bring exposure to books. Exposure generates sales. Sales mean more money in your pocket. Pursuing those book awards that allow publishers or authors to nominate their own titles can be a worthy investment.

Book awards influence buyers. When book buyers are presented with two books on the same topic and one is an award winner, book buyers consistently prefer the book that has won an award.

While entering a book award contest is not a guaranteed win for your entry fee, it certainly more than pays off if your book is picked for an award. Some book award programs publish the runners-up as well as the award winners. If your book falls into either of these categories, you receive a marketing gem.

Winning a book award provides a publisher with a number of benefits. One benefit of a book award is that it warrants press coverage. Newspapers, magazines, and newsletters like to highlight authors and books that have won awards. Another benefit of a book award is that consumers want to read books that have won awards. An award tells a consumer that a book is worth the money to purchase and the time to read it. An award also signals booksellers to purchase the book for their stores as book awards almost always guarantee sales.

Book awards, like book reviews, can be harnessed to promote your title in endless ways. When a book award is bestowed, the award should be used repeatedly in your marketing campaign. In addition to alerting the press about a book award, any book award should be posted on your website, printed on all your marketing materials, used in advertisements, and added to your book's cover on subsequent print runs. Also, make sure that you let your distributors know about the award and send an announcement to those publisher associations and discussion groups to which you belong.

Winning a book award warrants press coverage.

A book award itself does not sell your book. What it does is give your book credibility, which you can then use to sell more copies of your book. If you win a book award, be sure to make the most of it to gain as much publicity as you can for your book. In addition to the items listed above, be sure to do the following:

- Announce the award on all your social media sites (Facebook, Twitter, LinkedIn, etc.).
- Send an email to your existing email subscribers announcing the award.
- Update all the online listings for your book (Amazon.com, BarnesAndNoble.com, etc.) to reflect that the book has won a prestigious award.
- Add the information to your media kit and update your author biography to include the phrase "award-winning author."
- Order award stickers from the award organization and apply them to your book covers.
- Add the book award announcement to your email signature.
- Put the award on your letterhead and business cards.
- Hold a celebration party.

Many small publishers and self-publishers complain about the entry fees charged to nominate a book for an award, but you must remember that running a book award costs money. Unless an organization can find a corporate sponsor to underwrite an award, the organization hosting the book award must raise funds to support the award. This is most commonly done through entry fees. Entry fees also serve the purpose of ensuring that those entering the contest have thoroughly read the rules and determined that their book fits the nomination criteria presented in the award guidelines.

The literary community hosts a myriad of book awards. These awards differ as to who can nominate a book for an award. For some awards, publishers or authors can nominate their books and a committee or select group of people vote on the nominated titles. Other awards choose to have a nominating committee decide which titles should be considered for an award. Some awards have a select group of people (such as retailers, teachers, or students) nominate titles. There are a few book awards that are based on the number of copies a title has sold or lifetime achievements of an author. Generally, entry fees are charged for those awards that allow publishers and authors to nominate books.

Christian Book Awards

Christian book awards reflect the myriad of book awards available in the broader literary community. For some awards, publisher or author nomination is acceptable; for others, retailers nominate; and still others are based on sales figures.

- **American Academy of Religion Awards for Excellence**
  The American Academy of Religion (AAR) offers two Awards for Excellence: Best First Book in the History of Religions and Award for Excellence in the Study of Religion.

  The Best First Book in the History of Religions honors exceptional publications of first books published by nominees in the history of religion. Awards for Excellence in the Study of Religion recognize new works of books that affect decisively how religion is examined, understood, and interpreted. Awards in the Study of Religion are granted for four categories: Constructive-Reflective Study of Religion, Historical Studies, Textual Studies, and Analytical-Descriptive Study of Religion. Books can be nominated by any individual or institution.
  www.aarweb.org

- **Carol Awards**
  This award is given annually by American Christian Fiction Writers (ACFW) for Christian fiction works in 11 categories. Awards are given only for books whose authors are members of American Christian Fiction Writers. Entry rules and forms are available for members on ACFW's website.
  www.americanchristianfictionwriters.com

- **Catholic Press Awards**
  Presented annually by the Catholic Press Association (CPA), these Catholic book awards are given for 23 categories including First Time Author, Children's, Spirituality, Spanish-Language Book, and Best Book by a Small Publisher.
  www.catholicpress.org

- Christian Retailing's **Best Awards**
  This award, sponsored by *Christian Retailing*, is designed to recognize the most significant, life-changing products in the Christian industry. Nominations are accepted in 60 categories, but include games, toys, and gifts, as well as books. Christian retailers and others who work in the industry vote to determine the winners.
  http://christianretailingsbest.com

- **Christian Small Publisher Book of the Year Awards**
  This award is sponsored by Christian Small Publishers Association. The award is designed to both promote small publishers and independently published authors in the Christian marketplace as well as to bring recognition to outstanding books. To accomplish both of these goals, Christian Small Publishers Association has Christian retailers and readers vote on the books of their choice to determine the winners of the award. Awards are granted in 12 categories, including an ebook category.
  www.christianbookoftheyear.com

- *Christianity Today* **Book Awards**
  Presented annually by *Christianity Today* magazine, these awards honor titles in 10 categories. Books are judged on their contributions to bringing understanding to people, events, and ideas that shape evangelical life and mission.

Books are nominated by publishers. The staff of *Christianity Today* selects the top five books in each category and then panels of judges (one panel for each category) determine the winners.
www.christianitytoday.com

- **Christy Awards**
 The Christy Awards are presented annually to recognize and promote Christian fiction of an exceptional quality and impact. The awards feature nine fiction categories in which awards are presented, including General/Contemporary, Historical, Romance, Suspense/Mystery, Visionary, and First Novel. The entry submission deadline for the Christy Awards is in December for books published during that calendar year.
 www.christyawards.com

- **ECPA CHRISTIAN BOOK AWARD®**
 These annual awards are given by the Evangelical Christian Publishers Association (ECPA) in eight categories. They are designed to recognize the absolute highest quality in Christian books in the religious publishing community. Nominations can only be made by ECPA member publishers in good standing, who nominate their best books released in the previous calendar year.
 www.christianbookawards.com

- **ECPA Gold, Platinum, Diamond, & Double Diamond Sales Awards**
 Also awarded by ECPA, these book awards are based on sales figures for a title. They are designed to recognize outstanding sales achievement in the publication of quality Christian literature. Gold Book Awards are for books that have sold 500,000 copies, Platinum Book Awards are for titles which have achieved one million sales, Diamond Book Awards are for a book property selling ten million copies, and Double Diamond Book Awards are for when a book property sells 20 million copies. A book does not have to be published by an ECPA member publishing house to qualify for these awards.
 www.christianbookawards.com

- **Illumination Book Awards**
 This award is sponsored by the Jenkins Group, Inc. The Illumination Book Awards are designed to "shine a light" on the best new titles

written and published with a Christian worldview. Awards are granted in 16 categories including ebooks.
www.illuminationawards.com

- **Retailers Choice Awards**
Retailers Choice Awards are sponsored by *Christian Retailing*. Products nominated for the annual Retailers Choice Awards must have been published and released in the previous year. Nominations are accepted from publishers and then Christian retailers vote on the list of nominated titles. Votes are based on the impact the books have had on staff and customers, including a book's ability to speak to hearts and evoke emotion, open minds to new ways of thinking, and encourage and affirm Christ-like living.
www.retailerschoiceawards.com

- **Theologos Awards**
The Theologos Awards are given annually by the Association of Theological Booksellers (ATB) in five categories: Best General Interest Book, Best Academic Book, Best Children's Book, Book of the Year, and Publisher of the Year. Only bookseller members of the association are eligible to nominate and to vote.
http://associationoftheologicalbooksellers.org/theologos.html

General Book Awards with Religious Categories

A number of book awards exist in the general-market literary community that are aimed at the independent, small, or self-publisher. Most of these book awards include at least one religious category. Each of the awards listed below accepts nominations from publishers and/or authors.

- **Axiom Business Book Awards**
Presented by the Jenkins Group, Inc., the sponsor of the Independent Publisher Book Awards, the Axiom Business Book Awards are designed to increase the recognition of the very best business books and their creators. They offer 21 different categories of awards.
www.axiomawards.com

- **Ben Franklin Awards™**
  IBPA, The Independent Book Publishers Association, sponsors the Ben Franklin Awards, which are named in honor of America's most cherished publisher/printer. Books are judged on editorial and design merit by top practitioners in the field. Awards are presented for genre categories. Publishers must nominate titles.
  http://ibpabenjaminfranklinawards.com

- **The Eric Hoffer Award for Independent Books**
  These awards recognize extraordinary books by independent publishers. Awards in 18 categories, including ebooks, are offered.
  www.hofferaward.com

- *ForeWord Reviews* **Book of the Year Award**
  ForeWord Reviews Book of the Year Award was established to bring increased attention from librarians and booksellers to the literary achievements of independent publishers and their authors. The awards are presented in 60 categories including Religion and Religious Fiction. Print-on-demand titles and ebooks are accepted for nomination.
  www.bookoftheyearawards.com

- **Independent Publisher Book Awards**
  The Independent Publisher Book Awards are sponsored by the Jenkins Group, Inc. These awards are for independent, university, small press, and self-publishers who produce books intended for the North American market. The award offers 60 award categories, including Inspirational/Spiritual, Religious Fiction, and Religion, as well as 10 regional awards for fiction and nonfiction books. Books must have a copyright or have been released in the previous year to be eligible for nomination.
  www.independentpublisher.com

- **International Book Awards**
  Sponsored by USA Book News, these awards are offered in 150 categories including Children's Religious, Religious Fiction, Religion: Christianity, and Religion: Prayer & Devotional.
  www.internationalbookawards.com

- **Living Now Awards**
  Sponsored by the Jenkins Group (who also sponsors the Independent Publisher Awards, the Axiom Business Book Awards, and the Moonbeam Children's Awards). The Living Now Awards focus on best lifestyle and homestyle books, with 30 categories ranging from cooking and fitness to parenting and spirituality. They even have an Inspirational Fiction category.
  www.livingnowawards.com

- **Moonbeam Children's Book Award**
  This award is also sponsored by the Jenkins Group, Inc. The award is designed to bring increased recognition to exemplary children's books and their creators, and to support childhood literacy and lifelong reading. Awards are given in 40 categories.
  www.moonbeamawards.com

- **National Indie Excellence Awards**
  Open for all authors and publishers of books both national and international, these awards are presented in over 80 categories including Religion and Religious Fiction.
  www.indieexcellence.com

- **Readers Favorite Award**
  Sponsored by Readers Favorite, an online book review site, this award has no publication date requirements. They are open to manuscripts that have not been published as well as published works. Awards are offered in over 70 categories including nine Christian categories for both nonfiction and fiction titles.
  http://readersfavorite.com

- **ReaderViews Annual Literary Awards**
  These annual literary awards honor writers who self-published or had their books published by a subsidy publisher, small press, university press, or independent book publisher geared for the North American reading audience. Open for all authors and publishers of books both national and international, these awards are presented in over 46 categories including Religion.
  http://readerviews.com/literaryawards

- **The Nautilus Book Awards**
   These awards honor distinguished literary and heartfelt contributions to spiritual growth, conscious living, high-level wellness, green values, responsible leadership, and positive social change, as well as to the worlds of art, creativity and inspirational reading for children and young adults. Awards are offered in 20 categories including Religion.
   www.nautilusbookawards.com

- **The Next Generation Indie Book Awards®**
   This award is open to independent authors and publishers worldwide. It is the largest not-for-profit awards program for independent publishers. The award is offered in 60 categories including Religious Fiction and Religious Nonfiction.
   http://indiebookawards.com

- **Writer's Digest Self-Published Book Awards**
   Sponsored by Writer's Digest, these book are the only awards exclusively for self-published books. Awards are offered in nine categories.
   www.writersdigest.com/competitions

One Additional Award

There is one more award worth mentioning: The Mom's Choice Awards. This program recognizes authors, inventors, companies, and parents for their efforts in creating quality family-friendly media, products, and services. The award is especially interested in products that help families grow emotionally, physically, and spiritually; are morally sound and promote good will; and are inspirational and uplifting. Recognizing that moms make 85% of all buying decisions in a household, the Mom's Choice Awards is designed to give products a seal of approval that mothers recognize.

The Mom's Choice Awards (www.momschoiceawards.com) is really more of a "Seal of Approval" program than an award program. They grant their award to both books and products. This award has over 158 categories for books that they consider. All books published since 2008 are eligible. The nomination is open year round. The cost to nominate a book is $300. When a book is nominated, the Mom's Choice Awards judges make a decision within eight to twelve weeks of receiving the product.

Summary

Book awards abound in the literary community. Many general-market regional book publishers and bookseller associations also host awards for their member publishers' books. Many book festivals around the country also sponsor book awards. These local awards can be used to promote books just like the national awards. One independently published author of a children's book acquired over 12 awards for her book through entering multiple national and local book award contests.

8

Reach Christian Retailers

*And pray for us, too, that God may open a door
for our message, so that we may proclaim the mystery of Christ.*
—Colossians 4:3

> **Marketing Fundamental:**
> **Christian retail stores have an unlimited number
> of books vying for limited shelf space.**

The bottom line is that both the quantity and size of Christian retail stores are shrinking. First, when Christian titles became popular, big-box discount chains like Walmart® and Target® began to sell these books and took business away from the Christian bookstores. Then, as the Internet grew, sales of book migrated to the World Wide Web. Now, with digital book sales growing, many Christian retail stores struggle to maintain a viable presence.

With ever-increasing Internet connectedness and decreasing physical bookstore browsing, the way people discover books is shifting. As recently as two years ago, one-third of new books were discovered in physical bookstores. Now, that number has shrunk to one-fifth. In 2012, for the first time, online retail stores sold more books than brick-and-mortar retail stores in the United States. Last year, 44% of books bought by consumers were purchased online, while only 32% of books were purchased in large retail chains, independent bookstores, other mass merchandisers, and supermarkets.

All is not completely bleak for Christian retail stores. One industry report indicated that while 60% of Christian retailers suffered sales declines over the past few years, 40% saw sales increases. Another survey indicated that two-thirds of Christian retailers felt their store would still be in business in five years.

> Any given book has less than a 1% chance of being placed on a bookstore shelf.

One recent study found that Christian retail shoppers are voracious readers—spending more time weekly reading (three hours per week) in both print and digital formats than non-Christian bookstore shoppers (two hours per week). Since Christian retail shoppers are more committed to buying and reading books than most, getting your book in front of these consumers will lead to more sales.

Each year, bookstore buyers are presented with thousands of books to sell in their stores. For every available bookstore shelf space, there are 1,000 or more titles competing for that shelf space. In essence, any given book has less than a 1% chance of being placed on a bookstore shelf. Due to limited shelf space, booksellers must choose just a few hundred titles to stock in their stores each year. Which books get chosen? Retailer buyers choose those books by the best-known authors, those books that have the largest marketing campaigns, and those books that fill a special need their customers might have. What that boils down to is that, for most unknown authors, getting your books into a bookstore is extremely difficult. Unless you can show that your book is selling well, most stores won't stock it.

Before you approach Christian retailers about stocking your book, you must make sure that bookstores can order your book easily. This means that your books should be available through at least one of the major Christian distributors or wholesale book companies (listed in chapter 3). Be aware that most bookstores generally do not stock print-on-demand books.

Christian retailers are busy. They do not want to open small accounts with many different sources. Most Christian retailers order from a handful of sources for ease in accounting as well as reduced shipping fees (many of the larger distribution and wholesale companies offer free shipping with larger orders). Additionally, having your books available through established distribution channels signals to retailers that you are serious about marketing your books.

Should Christian retail stores choose not to stock your book, recognize that while these bookstores may not physically carry your book, this does not mean that someone can't order it from them. As long as your book is in the right distribution channels, customers can still request your book and bookstores can order it for the customer.

Remember, it never hurts to try, which is why this chapter looks at the most common and effective ways to let Christian booksellers know about your books.

BISAC

Pick up almost any book and on the back cover, either in the upper left-hand corner of the cover or near the EAN barcode, you will see classification words such as Fiction/Christian/Romance. These words are called BISAC subject headings or codes. The purpose of these subject headings is to give consumers, distributors, and booksellers a clear definition of a book's content. Subject headings let retailers know the best place to shelve the book in their stores. If you are serious about getting bookstores to stock your books, make sure each book has a subject heading on the back cover.

The Book Industry Standards and Communications (BISAC) subject codes are created by the Book Industry Study Group (BISG), a national, nonprofit organization committed to the development of effective industry-wide standards, best practices, research, and events related to both physical and digital products that enhance relationships between all trading partners. You can find a list of the current subject codes on BISG's website at www.bisg.org.

Industry Trade Shows

Industry trade shows are designed to let Christian booksellers know about new products while giving them an opportunity to get information on the latest trends and technology affecting their business. Publishers and other suppliers for the Christian retail marketplace exhibit their new products at these shows. Industry trade shows are mainly attended by Christian booksellers looking to acquire new products for their bookstores. The major Christian retail trade shows are listed on the following pages.

- **International Christian Retail Show (ICRS)**
  ICRS is the largest Christian retail industry trade show. Held annually each summer, this four-day show draws attendees from all over the world looking to acquire Christian products. Since the show is sponsored by CBA, The Association for Christian Retail, show exhibitors and attendees receive a discounted rate if they are members of CBA. Non-CBA member exhibitors must be approved by CBA prior to securing exhibit space. Recently, CBA has opened up some space for independent authors also to exhibit their books.
  www.christianretailshow.com

- **RBTE**
  RBTE stands for Religious Booksellers Trade Expo. This show is held annually around Memorial Day in Illinois. It is a gathering of the religious marketplace for Catholic, Episcopal, and other liturgical traditions. This show is very accessible for small publishers as they allow booth sharing.
  www.rbte.org

- **Christian Product Expo (CPE)**
  CPE is sponsored by the Munce Group for their member stores. The show is held for three days each September in Nashville, and each January in Hershey, Pennsylvania. Munce has recently added a one-day event to AmericasMart (the country's largest gift show for retailers). CPE is a tabletop show, meaning that the displays are centered on the products rather than around impressive signs and booth designs. This show is exclusively for Munce member retail stores and Munce pays for its member stores to attend the show if they write a minimum number of orders at the show.
  www.cpeshow.com

- **Catholic Marketing Network Trade Show**
  Catholic Marketing Network (CMN) hosts a CMN International Trade Show each August. This trade show is largely attended by Catholic book and gift stores, Catholic distributors, and Catholic media personnel. Only members of Catholic Marketing Network may exhibit at the trade show. Catholic Marketing Network retail members attend the trade shows free of charge. These shows are accessible for small publishers as CMN does allow booth sharing.
  www.catholicmarketing.com

Displaying at a Trade Show

In addition to bringing plenty of promotional materials (brochures, fliers, order forms) to a trade show, publishers exhibiting books should also plan to bring extra copies of the books they are displaying to give away as promotional titles. Providing free promotional copies of your books to media personnel, book reviewers, and chain bookstore buyers at trade shows is a sharp marketing tool. Having a "useful" promotional item to give freely to show attendees can generate long-term exposure to your products. Giving away bookmarks, pens, or magnets with your contact information printed on them will remind those individuals of your books on an ongoing basis and can result in additional sales.

Holding author book signings at trade shows is another good tool to bring Christian retail buyers' attention to your books. The majority of publishers host at least one author book signing for a new title at trade shows. Books signed by an author at trade shows are provided free of charge to retailers and other show attendees as author book signings are a promotional tool used to generate orders for the book from Christian retail stores.

Trade shows used to be the major forum through which bookstores placed orders for books. As more publishers have increased their use of sales representatives to sell books directly to bookstores, trade shows are no longer the main avenue through which booksellers order product. However, attendance at trade shows is still important for establishing a presence in the Christian marketplace and for forming relationships within the industry. New publishers can gain recognition and acceptance in the industry through creating a presence at trade shows.

Advertisements in Trade Journals

Publishers and suppliers can advertise their products to Christian retailers through trade journals aimed at the retail market. These journals give publishers another avenue to make their titles known to Christian retailers while encouraging them to stock the books in their stores.

Magazine advertisements do sell products. Look in any magazine and you will see that it is filled with advertisements. When you consider how vast the magazine industry is in America, it is evident that magazine advertisements work. If they did not, advertisements would not be driving the magazine industry and keeping magazines cost-effective for consumers. Remember, repetition is essential for selling with magazine advertisements.

Publishers have a few choices for advertising their books via trade journals to the Christian retail marketplace.

- **CBA Retailers + Resources**
  The official magazine of CBA, *CBA Retailers + Resources* is mailed free to all CBA members. Non-CBA members can pay for a subscription to the magazine. It is the only magazine in the industry written by retailers for retailers.
  Advertising is handled by Carl Dunn & Associates.
  Carl Dunn & Associates
  856-582-0690
  ellie@carldunn.com
  www.carldunn.com

- **Christian Retailing**
  Produced by Charisma Media, *Christian Retailing* is mailed free of charge to any retail bookstore in America that is actively selling Christian products. Subscriptions can be ordered by individuals and industry suppliers.
  For advertising information, contact Cliff Morales, Advertising Manager, at 407-333-0600 or cliff.morales@charismamedia.com.

- **CMN Marketplace News**
  The Catholic Marketing Network (CMN) does not produce a print newsletter for their retail members. Instead, they provide their members a regular e-newsletter. Authors and publishers can place advertisements in this digital newsletter to reach the Catholic retail members of the network with your products.
  Advertising information and rates can be obtained through contacting CMN.
  Catholic Marketing Network
  800-506-6333
  cmn@catholicmarketing.com
  www.catholicmarketing.com

Promotion Through Retail Marketing Groups

Many independent Christian retail stores are finding that they are unable to succeed in the marketplace as stand-alone stores. Retail marketing groups provide these stores with the networking and marketing support they need to remain viable in the current marketplace. Among their services, marketing groups offer their member stores marketing materials to hand out or mail to existing and potential customers. The majority of the cost of these materials is paid for by publishers placing advertisements for products in these promotional materials. Member retail stores then pay a small fee to purchase the materials for their use with customers.

Advertising in retail marketing groups' promotional materials can be an excellent use of advertising dollars. Retail marketing groups' catalogs fetch maximum exposure for your advertising dollar as they allow you to promote your titles to retail stores and consumers at the same time. Member retail stores are generally required to stock the items from the catalogs they distribute to their customers. This policy ensures that stores will carry your books when you advertise through this venue. One requirement for advertising in these retail marketing catalogs is that you must have your titles available through at least one of the three wholesale companies serving the Christian retail marketplace (see chapter 3).

Currently, five retail marketing groups provide opportunities for you to purchase advertisements in their promotional materials.

- **Catholic Marketing Network**

  The Catholic Marketing Network (CMN) produces seasonal catalogs that they mail free of charge to all of their member retail stores. These catalogs offer CMN's member stores a look at the latest products for the Catholic marketplace. Publishers do not need to be a member of CMN to advertise in the seasonal catalogs. CMN also sells advertising in their email blasts to their member retail stores.

  800-506-6333
  cmn@catholicmarketing.com
  www.catholicmarketing.com

- **Covenant Group**

  Covenant Group is an association of Christian retailers whose annual sales are over $500,000. It is run by retailers and operates for the benefit of its 80 member Christian stores. They offer two seasonal catalogs, eleven seasonal flyers, and an annual church supplies catalog.

  Covenant Group
  PO Box 170129
  1600 John B. White Blvd., Suite 1003
  Spartanburg, SC 29301
  864-587-2637
  www.covenantgroupstores.com

- **Munce Group**
    The Munce Group claims to be the nation's largest Christian full-service marketing group. Sporting over 400 Christian retail members, the Munce Group offers seasonal catalogs and flyers for their member stores. Member stores are required to participate in the spring and Christmas catalogs. Most member retailers participate in four to six promotions each year. These catalogs reach millions of consumers.

    Contact Sue Brewer at sue.brewer@munce.com for more information on advertising with the Munce Group.

    Munce Group
    200 West Bay Drive
    Largo, FL 33770
    800-868-4388
    www.munce.com

- **The Parable Group**
    The Parable Group provides marketing services for over 100 member stores. They offer seasonal catalogs and flyers to their member stores. Products featured in Parable's catalogs and flyers are chosen at regularly scheduled presentation meetings. Publishers and other vendors who have completed an application process present products to a selection board comprised of store owners, buyers, and staff. These boards select products best suited to meet the needs of Parable's customers.

    Contact Randy Ross at randy.ross@parable.com or 805-543-2644 for more information on advertising with the Parable Group.

    The Parable Group
    102 Cross Street, Suite 210
    San Luis Obispo, CA 93401
    (800) 366-6031
    www.parablegroup.com

- **Logos Bookstore Association**
    A group of independently owned and operated Christian bookstores in the United States and Canada, Logos Bookstore Association is the smallest of the retail marketing groups. The 18 member stores in this association carry a core of product in common but each store also has the ability to reflect the needs of its community in choice of additional products. The Logos Bookstore Association produces two seasonal catalogs for their member stores.

Logos Bookstore Association offers publishers an additional way to tell its member stores about your products: a weekly email for its member stores. This email contains news, prayer requests, and vendor specials. Send them your new book announcements and special offers to be listed in this e-newsletter.

Contact Rebecca Gorczyca at becky@logosbookstores.com or Sue Labrie at sue.labrie@logosbookstores.com for announcements or advertising in Logos catalogs.

Logos Bookstore Association
1675 East Main St. #204
Kent, OH 44240
330-677-8086
www.logosbookstore.com

Advertising Through Your Distributor

All the major Christian distributors have advertising programs that target bookstores. These distributors create print seasonal catalogs that are sent to bookstores. They also have e-newsletters and eblasts that authors and publishers can advertise in. These catalogs and emails provide another avenue to get your products in front of bookstore buyers and decision makers. Check with your distributor to find out more about specific catalogs and mailings that are available for you to participate in.

Direct Mail Campaigns

A direct-mail or email campaign to reach Christian retail stores is another marketing option. However, direct mail campaigns tend not to be as successful as advertising in trade journals or consumer catalogs geared to Christian retailers. With thousands of Christian books published each year, booksellers are overwhelmed with choices of what to carry in their stores. The typical Christian retailer buys from a select handful of publishers. As a result, unsolicited mail or email that comes across a book buyer's desk generally receives the least amount of attention.

Christian retail shoppers are voracious readers.

The average response rate on direct mail marketing is one to two percent of your mailing. However, if you have a unique marketing angle or a book by a known Christian personality, the response rate from direct mail can be higher than the average. Three main organizations rent mailing lists of Christian retail stores.

- **CBA, The Association for Christian Retail**
CBA offers three different U.S. Christian retail mailing lists: CBA Member Stores List, Non-member Stores List, and a Combined CBA Member / Non-member List. The combined list features a total of 2200 Christian retail outlets in the United States. CBA offers these rental mailing lists in a single-use format. The association must pre-approve your sample mailing before you can purchase a list. CBA also offers these same lists in a database format for CBA member publishers who want to use the addresses repeatedly for mailing. Of course, the price for the database is much higher than for the list rental.

CBA also offers eblasts to their list of 2400 individual retailer locations, but the price is not cheap.

CBA
9240 Explorer Drive, Suite 200
Colorado Springs, CO 80920
719-265-9895
info@cbaonline.org
www.cbaonline.org/nm/MarketProduct.htm

- **Association of Catholic Publishers (ACP)**
ACP maintains a mailing list of approximately 1124 Catholic bookstores. The list is available on a one-time rental basis. Members of ACP receive a discounted rate for the mailing list.

Association of Catholic Publishers
410-988-2926
info@catholicpublishers.org
www.catholicpublishers.org

- **Christian Retailing**
Charisma Media, the producer of *Christian Retailing* magazine, offers rental mailing lists of Christian stores. They also offer eblasts to Christian stores for a fee.

David Manning, List Rental Manager
407-333-0600
david.manning@charismamedia.com

- **Episcopal Booksellers Association, Inc.**
  The Episcopal Booksellers Association is made up of around 80 Episcopal bookstores across the United States and Canada. This association publishes an annual membership directory. Supporting vendor members are given a copy of the membership directory and may utilize this directory for conducting direct mailings.
  Debbie Whittemore, Executive Director
  888-589-8020
  ExecDirec@episcopalbooksellers.org
  www.episcopalbooksellers.org

Direct Sales

Sales representatives making personal sales calls to bookstore buyers is one of the most effective sales techniques in selling books to retail stores. However, most small and self-publishers cannot afford to pay sales representatives to traverse the country and make personal calls to Christian bookstore buyers. Apart from national sales representation, small publishers should at least make sales calls to those chain bookstores with buyers headquartered in your locale as well as the larger independent bookstores located in your corner of the country.

For a listing of member CBA Christian stores in your state, visit http://cba.know-where.com/cba.

Most of the larger Christian retail chain stores will review new products from small publishers to determine if these products fit into their current product mix. These chain stores allow small publishers to submit new products for review. When submitting products for review to a chain bookstore's headquarters, you should include your marketing plans, book reviews garnered, and the distributors that carry your books. Most chains will not consider a submitted product that is not available through either Spring Arbor, Anchor Distributors, or Send The Light (see chapter 3).

The number of chain Christian retail stores is dwindling as many have merged. Following is a listing of the major Christian chain bookstores.

- **Family Christian Stores®**
  Family Christian Stores is the largest chain of Christian bookstores in the United States. They operate 285 stores. They now run a commission sales model, meaning that they only pay for the product that they sell.

As such, they do not order product from distributors or wholesalers, but work with a select group of publishers who give them product to carry on a commission basis. Product submission guidelines are on their website.

Family Christian Stores / A-5
5300 Patterson Ave. SE
Grand Rapids, MI 49530
www.familychristian.com/productreview

- **LifeWay® Christian Stores**

LifeWay Christian Resources of the Southern Baptist Convention owns and operates 180 LifeWay Christian Stores throughout the United States. LifeWay produces a consumer catalog that their member stores utilize as a marketing tool. Small publishers can advertise their products in this catalog. Products that are advertised in the catalog are carried by the LifeWay Christian Stores. Information on advertising in the LifeWay catalog and contact information can be found on their website.

If you are interested in submitting a product for LifeWay to consider, they ask that you first submit your request in writing. Once your request has been reviewed, they will send you a reply with instruction and details explaining their process. Submit your request to newproducts@lifeway.com.

LifeWay Christian Stores
One LifeWay Plaza
Nashville, TN 37234-0162
www.lifeway.com

- **Mardel®, Inc.**

Mardel operates 35 stores. Information on how to submit product for review to Mardel is on the company's website.

Mardel, Inc.
attn: Book Buyer
7727 SW 44th St.
Oklahoma City, OK 73179
888-262-7335
www.mardel.com/authors

Online Christian Bookstores

Over the past few years, the number of books purchased over the Internet has rapidly grown, so having your book listed in the larger online bookstores is important. Other than Amazon.com and BarnesAndNoble.com, listing a book in the larger Christian online bookstores can provide consumers easier access to ordering your book.

Following is a listing of some of the larger online Christian bookstores.

- **Christian Book Distributors (CBD)**
  Christian Book Distributors is a large online store for Christian products. As an independently published author or small publisher, it is difficult to get CBD to pick up your books for their online store. However, if your books are listed with a Christian distributor (see chapter 3), then generally, CBD will include the books on their website.
  Christian Book Distributors
  PO Box 7000
  Peabody, MA 01961-7000
  800-247-4784
  www.christianbook.com

- **Cokesbury Bookstores**
  Cokesbury is the retail division of the United Methodist Publishing House. At one time, it operated close to 100 retail stores across the United States. However, more recently, Cokesbury closed all their physical retail outlets and went to an online-only format. To submit product for review to Cokesbury, contact their headquarters first to determine the category buyer to which your books should be sent.
  Cokesbury Bookstores
  201 Eighth Ave. S.
  PO Box 801
  Nashville, TN 37202
  800-672-1789
  cokes_serv@cokesbury.com
  www.cokesbury.com

- **DeeperCalling Media, LLC**
  DeeperCalling Media provides online bookstores for close to 1000 Christian and secular booksellers through DeeperShopping.com.

If your book is made available for the book trade through one of the Christian distributors, then DeeperCalling will automatically feature your book on their DeeperShopping website. For those who have not secured distribution, DeeperCalling has a consignment program through which you can apply to have your print book on their website.

They also feature ebooks on their site, and any author or publisher can register an account and upload their ebooks for listing on the site. All information regarding how to have DeeperCalling Media carry your books is provided on their website.

DeeperCalling Media, LLC
4280 Brogdon Exchange, Suite B
Suwanee, GA 30024
888 372 0011
www.deepercalling.com

Summary

Sales through Christian bookstores account for about half of Christian book sales. Keeping Christian retail a viable entity benefits all publishers publishing materials for the Christian marketplace since Christian bookstores carry the largest selection of Christian materials of any brick-and-mortar retail outlet.

While the majority of a Christian small publisher's book sales may not come directly through Christian retail stores, this market is still an important avenue in making your books available to Christian consumers. A number of Christian consumers are loyal to their local Christian bookstore. When these individuals hear about a new book, they prefer to purchase the book through their local Christian bookstore. A marketing campaign that includes Christian retail stores can serve to bring additional sales for your books.

Connect with Churches

Preach the Word; be prepared in season and out of season; correct, rebuke and encourage— with great patience and careful instruction.
—2 Timothy 4:2

> Marketing Fundamental:
> **Reach church leaders
> and you reach the people.**

Hundreds of thousands of churches exist in the United States representing over 1,000 different church denominations, most of which can be sorted into 15 main denominational families based on their historical roots. Currently, the denominational families with the most members are Catholic, Baptist, Methodist/Wesleyan, Lutheran, Presbyterian, Pentecostal/Charismatic, and Anglican/ Episcopalian. These churches, collectively, have thousands of leaders shepherding their congregations.

Each church in America represents numerous Christian consumers. In a 2012 survey, the Pew Research Council found that 48% of the population in the United States identified themselves as Protestant (150.7 million) and 22% identified themselves as Catholic (69 million). Churches provide a number of different opportunities for you to promote your books to Christian readers.

Church Libraries

While the trend for many Christian churches is to offer retail Christian book sales, a large proportion of churches still host church libraries. Hence church libraries remain a prominent avenue for book sales. Conservative estimates place church libraries at 50,000 across the United States. These libraries can be as small as a single bookshelf or as large as an entire room in a church. Most have a designated librarian who is in charge of library maintenance and purchasing materials.

> One in three Christians have purchased a product after hearing about it during a sermon.

One effective method for marketing to a large number of church libraries is through a church library association. Most church library associations hold an annual convention for their members. These conventions provide publishers opportunities to exhibit their books and place promotional inserts in the convention program packets for reasonable fees. Church library associations also publish regular newsletters or journals for their members. These newsletters print reviews of Christian products and some include paid advertisements, providing more avenues for you to promote your titles.

Some of these associations also rent mailing lists of their member libraries. You can use these lists to conduct a targeted mailing to further promote your books to church libraries.

The primary church library associations are listed here.

- **Catholic Library Association (CLA)**
  CLA is an international organization for Catholic church and school libraries. Their quarterly publication, *Catholic Library World*, features book reviews and advertising. CLA's annual convention is held in conjunction with the National Catholic Education Association's (NCEA) annual convention.
  www.cathla.org

- **Church and Synagogue Library Association (CSLA)**
  CSLA publishes a quarterly publication, *Congregational Libraries Today*. This publication features reviews of new materials. CSLA also holds an annual national conference.
  http://cslainfo.org

- **The Evangelical Church Library Association (ECLA)**
  ECLA is a national library association for church and Christian school librarians. They produce a quarterly publication, *Church Libraries*, which features advertisements and dedicates about 75% of its material to reviews. ECLA hosts a convention in Wheaton, Illinois, each year.
  www.eclalibraries.org

- **Pacific Northwest Association of Church Libraries (PNACL)**
  PNACL is a regional association for church libraries in the Pacific Northwest (Washington, Oregon, and Idaho). They host an annual conference and publish a quarterly newsletter, *The Lamplighter*, which features reviews of books.
  www.pnacl.org

Church Leaders

As might be expected, Church leaders read Christian books. A study by the Barna Group found that although the typical Protestant pastor makes less than the average household income, these pastors rank among the top ten percent of book buyers in America. Almost all of these pastors (98%) had purchased at least one book in the past year and the typical pastor bought 20 volumes in that time frame. One out of every five pastors purchased 50 or more titles in one year, an average of about one book per week!

Church leaders are influential. Senior pastors, associate pastors, youth pastors, children's ministers, Sunday school teachers, small group Bible study leaders, and women's ministry leaders are all individuals within a church who hold the authority to recommend books to church attendees. Surveys show that many people take the recommendations of their church leaders when it comes to what books to read and buy. Nine out of ten Protestant pastors make book recommendations from the pulpit.

Barna Research has found that church worship services are a major source of recommendations about Christian products. Nearly one in three Christians have purchased a Christian product after hearing about it in a sermon in a church and one in six have made a purchase after hearing about it on the radio. Generally, if a pastor recommends something from the pulpit, people buy it. Even Sunday school teachers' and Bible study leaders' recommendations motivate people to purchase and read books.

A number of avenues are available for you to promote your books to church leaders.

Church Denominations

For authors or publishers who are strongly aligned with a church denomination, a good marketing strategy is to promote your titles through your denomination. Church denominations have many avenues for you to promote titles. Most denominations have national and regional conferences for their various church leaders. Many have regular publications that feature advertisements, announcements, and even product reviews that are sent to member churches. Some denominations host their own web-based bookstore for their churches' leaders and members. Member church directories or mailing lists can often be obtained from the denominational headquarters for direct mailings. Making personal contact with the denominational head of the department within the church you are trying to reach (e.g., women's ministries, children's ministries, youth pastors, etc.) could garner a promotion of your book within that department of the denomination.

> Pastors rank among the top ten percent of book buyers.

The best way to find out which opportunities exist to promote your titles through any church denomination is to visit the denomination's main website. Since there are too many church denominations to feature adequately here (a whole book could be devoted just to church denominations), below is a sampling of two church denominations with some of the promotional opportunities they provide.

- **Presbyterian Church in America (PCA)**
  PCA holds an annual national assembly for church leaders and members featuring an exhibit hall. Their Christian Education and Publications division hosts a "Women in the Church Leadership Training Conference" for women who want to be lay leaders in the church. They also hold an annual Children's Ministry Conference. This division also features an online Christian education and publications

bookstore for church leaders. An online directory of member churches by state and a print version of their member church directory are also available. PCA's Christian Education and Publications division has its own website separate from the main PCA website. The Christian Education and Publication division's website is www.pcacep.org.
www.pcanet.org

- **Free Methodist Church**
The Free Methodist Church holds annual regional conferences for their church leaders. They produce *Light & Life*, a bimonthly magazine with a circulation of 55,000 (mostly to Free Methodist church members), featuring articles and advertisements. The denomination's website features reviews of books of interest to pastors. An international women's ministry featuring an annual conference and regular newsletter is also part of the denomination. The church's website hosts an online directory of member churches by state.
http://fmcusa.org

Church Leaders' Conferences

Most church denominations host conferences for their pastors. Information about these conferences is generally located on the denomination's website.

There are also a number of national and regional church leadership conferences that are nondenominational in nature. These conferences draw from a wide range of churches. Conferences exist for pastors, youth pastors, and Christian education leaders. Many opportunities exist within these conferences to reach church leaders. Publishers can exhibit products or place promotional materials in the conference packets that are handed out to conference attendees. Some conferences allow advertising in their conference programs and others allow publishers to have authors speak on their books' topics in a seminar. Below is a list of nondenominational church conferences. It is by no means comprehensive, but serves as a sampling of what is available for marketing books to church leaders.

Pastor Conferences: If you have a book a church pastor would be interested in, consider this type of conference to reach pastors with your product. Remember, if a pastor likes a book and recommends it to his congregation, church members will purchase and read it. Two national conferences geared toward pastors are The National Conference for Catechetical Leadership (www.nccl.us) and the ReFocus Moody's Pastor Conference (www.moodyconferences.com).

Youth Pastor Conferences: Connecting with youth pastors is a good way to get your book in the hands of teens. Youth pastors often recommend good books to their youth groups. Youth Specialties hosts National Youth Workers Conventions (http://nywc.com) regionally around the country. The National Federation for Catholic Youth Ministries (www.nfcym.org) also holds an annual conference for Catholic youth and youth leaders.

Children's Pastor Conferences: Churches stock their Sunday school and child care rooms with resources for the children and teachers. These resources include books for the children to look at and read. Marketing to children's pastors can result in churches' ordering your products for their children's rooms. Parents, in turn, are exposed to the books and may purchase them for their children. Children's pastors also often recommend good books to parents for educating their children in the faith.

One good way to reach a large number of children's pastors is through a conference for this group. The International Network of Children's Ministry (www.incm.org) holds International Children's Pastors Conferences annually at different locations around the United States.

Christian Education Conferences: Most nondenominational Christian education conferences geared toward adult and children's ministry leaders are held in regional or state locations in the spring. Many Christian education conferences are small, drawing just from their surrounding area. However, some of these conferences are regional in scope and boast higher attendances. These include:

- **BASS Church Workers Convention**
  www.bassconvention.org

- **Christian Education Association**
  www.christianeducationassn.org

- **Christian Ministries Training Association (CMTA)**
  www.cmtaconvention.org

- **National Capital Christian Education Conference**
  www.gwcea.org

- **Northwest Ministry Conference in Washington State**
  www.ministryconference.org

- **Religious Education Congress in California**
  www.recongress.org

- **Western Christian Educator's Conference**
  www.westernceconf.org

Direct Mail

One technique to gain the attention of church leaders for your titles is to generate your own postcard, flier, or brochure and conduct a direct mailing. Church mailing lists can be obtained from various organizations. Many church mailing lists can be ordered according to denomination, church size, ethnic churches, or by church ministry. Some companies that provide church mailing lists also offer an introductory rate for new users to test market a portion of a mailing list.

Four good sources for church mailing lists are:

- **The Church Ladies**
  www.churchladies.com

- **Tri-Media Marketing Services**
  www.trimediaonline.com

- **American Church Lists**
  www.americanchurchlists.com

- **The Official Catholic Directory**
  www.officialcatholicdirectory.com

A direct snail-mail campaign can be costly. A cheaper direct mail option for promoting your titles to church leaders is advertising in a card pack. Direct mailing service companies print promotional cards for businesses and then mail packets containing these cards to pastors and churches. Card packs can be much more cost effective than direct mail. Research figures indicate that advertising in a card pack can cost up to 75% less than a solo mailing. Many promotional card pack services also offer introductory rates so that advertisers can test the market. Tri-Media Marketing Services offers quarterly Pastors Info Packets (www.trimediaonline.com).

Sarah Bolme

Email Blasts

Another way to reach church leaders is through dedicated email blasts. While email campaigns are generally less expensive than snail mail campaigns, emails are easier to delete without scanning or reading than paper fliers. Four services that offer the ability to purchase an email blast via their established lists are:

- The Church Ladies
  www.churchladies.com

- Tri-Media Marketing Services
  www.trimediaonline.com

- Outreach Media Group
  www.outreachmediagroup.com

- The Official Catholic Directory
  www.officialcatholicdirectory.com

Advertising in Magazines and Journals

Placing advertisements in magazines and journals that target various church leaders can enhance your marketing campaign to churches. Another option is to get free coverage through submitting articles to magazines or journals that provide church leaders with useful information. Using an excerpt from the book you wish to promote is one great way to gain church leaders' attention for your title.

The Christian Writer's Market Guide is an invaluable resource for locating magazines and journals targeted to various church leaders. This book (which is updated annually) features both topical and target market alphabetical listings of periodicals and e-zines for the Christian marketplace and includes publications specifically geared for church leaders.

Creative Marketing

Innovative thinking can lead to effective marketing in reaching church leaders with your books. For example, there are retreat centers around the country that cater to pastors who need to rest body and soul and have a renewal experience. One creative marketing idea is to make gift copies of a book you have published (one that could be an encouragement resource for pastors or their wives) available to the pastoral couples using such a retreat. When making promotional copies available free of charge in this manner, remember to include a letter with the book that tells the recipient that this copy of the book is a gift from you. Also include information on how to order additional copies as well as how to schedule the author for a speaking engagement.

You can find lists of retreat centers that open their doors to pastors on the following websites:

- www.my-pastor.com/pastor-retreat-centers.html
- www.lawrencewilson.com/free-retreats-vacations-pastors
- http://enrichmentjournal.ag.org/retreats.pdf

Summary

Reach the leaders and you reach the people. Usually, if a pastor recommends something from the pulpit, people buy it. Reaching people in churches and engaging church leaders to help you spread the word about your books is one way to enlarge your marketing reach.

Partner with Christian Organizations

*Two are better than one, because
they have a good return for their labor.*
—Ecclesiastes 4:9

> Marketing Fundamental:
> **Partnering extends your marketing reach.**

Selling direct to consumers and through retail channels often results in a constant trickle of book sales that adds up over time. However, more than half of all book sales are made in non-bookstore outlets. Publishers looking to maximize book sales should pursue special sales. Special sales are quantity sales made outside of bookstores to a single entity—usually a catalog company, a corporation, a school, or other nonprofit organization—at a discount.

Partnering with Christian organizations allows publishers and authors to often secure large quantity non-returnable sales. Moreover, even if you don't secure large-scale sales agreements, partnering with these entities still gives you the ability to promote your books to a niche market, which can reel in more sales.

Mail-Order Catalogs

There are over 9,000 consumer mail-order catalogs in the United States. There are catalogs for just about every interest: gardening, baby, Christmas, clothing, gift, craft, pet supplies, etc. Catalog companies are always looking for new products to include in the next edition of their catalog. While few catalogs are devoted exclusively to books, many mail-order catalogs include books that are relevant to their topic.

Finding a mail-order catalog to carry your book provides you free exposure to thousands, maybe even millions, of consumers. Catalog companies usually order large quantities so that they can have the stock on hand to ship to their customers. While catalog companies purchase products at a fairly high discount, the sales are generally non-returnable and usually the catalog company pays the shipping.

> More than half of all book sales are made in non-bookstore outlets

Of course, as a Christian author or publisher, you do not need to limit your mail-order catalog selection to just Christian-themed catalogs. Many catalogs that reach the general market also carry religious materials since most catalog publishers realize that a large portion of their clientele holds religious beliefs.

There are a number of resources available to find mail-order catalog companies. Most of the resources list the catalogs by product area; for example, food and beverage, toys and games, health and personal care, etc. Here is a great resource to locate mail-order catalog companies that might be a match for your books:

- *The Directory of Mail Order Catalogs*
  This publication costs about $250.00 and lists both consumer and business catalogs. You might be able to find it in your public library.

There are also a few catalog search engines online geared toward consumers who shop using catalogs. You can use these sites to search for catalogs when looking for matches for your products. However, these search engines are not exhaustive lists and do not provide the same information as the paid directories.

— Sarah Bolme —

These free catalog search sites include:

- www.catalogs.com
- www.cataloglink.com
- www.buyersindex.com
- www.mail-order-catalogs.info
- www.cybercatalogs.com

Christian Catalogs

The following three catalogs are a good starting place for those seeking to secure space in Christian-themed mail-order catalogs.

- **Catholic Child**
  Catholic Child Catalog is the geared for Catholic youth of all ages, toddler through young adult.
  Catholic Child
  Product Submissions
  PO Box 298
  Petaluma, CA 94953
  www.catholicchild.com

- **Christian Book Distributors (CBD)**
  CBD is the world's largest mail-order catalog company.
  Christian Book Distributors
  140 Summit St.
  Peabody, MA 01960
  www.christianbooks.com

- **Christian Tools of Affirmation (CTA)**
  CTA provides purposeful products to help encourage God's people. The catalog features mostly gift products, but books that make good gifts are also included.
  CTA, Inc.
  1625 Larkin Williams Rd.
  PO Box 1205
  Fenton, MO 63026
  www.ctainc.com

Christian Charities

Christian charities abound. These nonprofit organizations provide services to just about every population group and problem that exists. Christian charities exist through donations, largely from individual donors. These organizations want to give their donors incentives to keep giving money. Many offer a product (often a Christian book) for a "suggested donation" amount. Nonprofits purchase these products for less than the charity's suggested donation. While some donors send in just the suggested amount to get the item; many donors send in larger amounts. This is what the organization is counting on; a giveaway product that brings them increased donations. Pursuing book sales to Christian charitable organizations is effort that is likely to reap sales of books.

To secure sales for a Christian charity, first determine what population an organization would serve that might fit well with the topic of your book. For example, if your book is a story of one woman's struggle to become free of domestic violence, then consider Christian-based domestic violence programs. If you have a missionary story, consider mission organizations. Most Christians tend to think of the large charitable organizations such as World Vision, Compassion, Focus on the Family, Prison Fellowship, etc., when this subject is broached. However, if you are a smaller Christian publisher, think outside the box and consider smaller, lesser-known charitable organizations to sell books to.

To find Christian charities, begin with an online search for the kind of charity you are looking for and see what comes up. Another way to search for charitable organizations is to visit www.taxexemptworld.com or www.nonprofitdata.com. Both of these websites allow you to look up IRS-registered nonprofit organizations by state, county, city, or zip code. Often a large number of nonprofit organizations will be displayed and you will have to search through the list to find Christian charities that serve your identified population.

Once you have identified a few charitable organizations, your next step is to approach each organization about the possibility of purchasing your book to use in their marketing and fund-raising efforts. If you have not done this type of sales before, start with a smaller local nonprofit. Make sure you include how the book is a good fit for the organization and why the organization's donor base would be interested in and benefit from your book when making your pitch. Be prepared to give a discount (at least 50%) for orders of 100 books or more and to change your book's cover and even add the nonprofit's logo and mission statement to the book's cover if the nonprofit organization requests.

Christian Organizations

Christian organizations and associations exist for every group of people: mothers, fathers, women, men, military, disabled, farmers, and nurses, to name a few. Whatever your target market, a Christian organization already exists that provides support and services to this demographic. Many opportunities exist for marketing your books through these Christian organizations.

Most of these organizations hold national or regional conferences where publishers can exhibit books or advertise in conference publications. All provide some type of publication to their members or target group that publishes articles and displays ads. Some provide their members an online store or catalog from which to purchase materials that speak to their unique situation. You can find economical ways to market through these organizations to reach large numbers of your target audience.

The number of Christian organizations that exist is astounding. Most secular associations have a Christian counterpart. For example, for the secular International Association of Firefighters (www.iaff.org), the counterpart is the Fellowship of Christian Firefighters International (http://fellowshipofchristianfirefighters.com).

The following list is by no means comprehensive. It is a partial list of some of the many Christian associations that authors and publishers can target if you have a book that fits the professionals a particular association serves.

- **American Association of Christian Counselors (AACC)**
  AACC is a professional association that assists Christian counselors and pastors to equip them with Biblical truth and psychosocial insights that minister to hurting persons.
  www.aacc.net

- **CBMC International**
  CBMC International serves and encourages business and professional marketplace leaders to share the Good News with others in the workplace, resulting in lasting life change.
  www.cbmcint.org

- **Christian Legal Society (CLS)**
  CLS is a national nondenominational organization of attorneys, judges, law professors, and law students, working in association with others, to follow Jesus' command "to do justice with the love of God."
  www.clsnet.org

- **Christian Medical & Dental Associations (CMDA)**
  CMDA provides resources, networking opportunities, education, and a public voice for Christian healthcare professionals and students.
  www.cmda.org

- **The Fellowship of Christian Athletes (FCA)**
  FCA is the largest Christian sports organization in America.
  www.fca.org

- **MOPS™**
  MOPS stands for Mothers of Preschoolers, and ministers to mothers of preschool-aged children in small groups around the country.
  www.mops.org

- **North American Association of Christians in Social Work (NACSW)**
  NACSW equips its members to integrate Christian faith and professional social work practice.
  www.nacsw.org

- **Nurses Christian Fellowship**
  This organization, under InterVarsity, is a professional organization for Christian nurses.
  http://ncf-jcn.org

- **Promise Keepers**
  This organization helps men live Godly lives.
  www.promisekeepers.org

Lists of Christian organizations are difficult to find on the Internet. It is best just to use a search engine to search for the type of organization you are looking for. One place that does provide a list of some Christian organizations (although it is an older list) is www.iclnet.org/pub/resources/xn-dir2.html.

Christians in the Military

Christians can be found in almost every profession that exists. The military is no exception. While a 2008 study of U.S. military members found that members of the military are less likely to be Christian than the general

U.S. population, a large percentage of military enlistees still consider themselves to be Christian. The U.S. general population self-reports around 80% Christian, while, according to the 2008 study, the military services (combined) self-report about 77% Christian.

This figure is still a large majority of the military. According to Wikipedia, the United States has the second-largest military in the world. At about 1,430,000 military personnel, the United States is second only to China. If 77% of these military personnel consider themselves to be Christians, that is over one million potential readers for your Christian books. This figure does not include the wives and other family members of these Christian military personnel.

Many authors and publishers have found that it is very difficult to get their books into the military markets, not because the military doesn't order Christian books, but because it is a time-consuming and cumbersome project that includes complex purchasing rules and regulations. For example, while commissaries (military grocery stores) don't carry books, military exchanges do. One main distributor to military exchanges is TNG (www.tng.com). However, TNG does not buy direct from self-publishers or those publishers with fewer than five books in print.

Associations Serving Christian Military Personnel

Given the difficulty of selling books directly into the military market, small publishers can still get their titles in front of military personnel. However, doing so may take some different strategies than your usual book promotional techniques. One way to reach Christian military personnel with your titles is to tap into the associations that serve Christian military personnel and use their vehicles for communication to highlight your titles. Consider the following associations and the opportunities they offer for your titles that would benefit military personnel and their families' members.

- **Officers' Christian Fellowship (OCF)**
  OCF is an association for officers in the military. Their purpose is to glorify God by uniting Christian officers for Biblical fellowship and outreach, equipping and encouraging them to minister effectively in the military society.

  This fellowship publishes a bimonthly publication called *Command Magazine*. While the magazine does not feature advertising, it does feature articles. There is a list of article topics the magazine is looking for on the fellowship's website. Their article topics are not all just related directly to military service. They use articles on such topics as time management, marriage and parenting, and personal faith. Another idea is to have a military officer you know write a review of the book for the magazine.

In addition, the OCF operates two conference centers for military leaders and their families. Most conference centers host small gift shops. If your book is a good fit for military leaders or you have published a book by a current or ex-military officer, contact these conference centers to find out how you might get your book into their gift shops.

www.ocfusa.org

- **Association for Christian Conferences, Teaching, and Service (ACCTS)**
ACCTS exits to assist in the development of Christian leaders in the armed forces of the world and in the establishment and growth of military Christian fellowships. The organization publishes an online magazine *Journal of Faith & War* (http://faithandwar.org) and sponsors conferences.

    www.accts.org

- **Christian Military Wives (CMW)**
CMW's mission is to assist military wives and their families through encouragement and education. The site has a blog were members can submit blog posts. If you have a book that military moms would find useful, finding a member of the CMW to review your book and blog about it on the CMW blog would bring some good exposure.

    www.cmwives.org

Military Libraries

Another way to reach military personnel with your titles is to get military libraries to purchase copies of your books. The military operates hundreds of libraries on their bases. The Special Librarian Association has a Military Libraries Division, which can be found at http://military.sla.org. This division hosts a Military Libraries Workshop (MLW) each year with tabletop exhibits, allowing you an opportunity to introduce your titles to military library buyers.

Christian Schools

Over five million students in the United States, about one of every ten children, attend private schools; most of them Christian. That is a lot of students and a lot of schools that could be purchasing your books. Schools buy all sorts of materials beyond curricula. Most classrooms sport supplemental reading material (i.e., books) and school libraries are stocked with fun as well as educational books. Families also purchase books and each student in a Christian school is part of a family representing more potential book sales.

There are Christian schools in every community across the United States, representing hundreds of thousands of reading children, their families, and their teachers, which provide opportunities for you to market your books.

Book Fairs

Many Christian schools hold book fairs where students, teachers, and parents can purchase books. These book fairs raise money for the school as well as provide the students and their families with quality reading material. You can submit your books for consideration to companies that provide book fair services to Christian schools. Some book fair companies provide a range of books from many publishers. Two of the general market book fair companies that provide services to religious schools include:

- **Mrs. Nelson's Book Fair Company**
  Mrs. Nelson's book fairs are offered in California and include Catholic and Evangelical schools.
  www.mrsnelsons.com

- **Books Are Fun**
  Through their nationwide network of independent sales representatives, Books Are Fun offers great book and gift products at amazing prices to schools, hospitals and corporations across the country.
  www.booksarefun.com

Speaking at Local Schools

Teachers love speakers; especially free speakers. Speakers mean that the teacher does not have to be the authority on every subject. Elementary school teachers enjoy hosting local authors to read their book to their students, which allows the students to meet an actual author. Middle and high school teachers often supplement their classroom material with speakers who are experts in a particular subject.

To secure speaking engagements in local Christian schools, begin by contacting the schools in an author's area and letting them know about the author's books and availability to speak to classes. When a speaking opportunity is secured, be sure to provide the author with plenty of promotional materials to leave with the teacher and the children. For elementary-aged children, bookmarks featuring the author's book and ordering information are great marketing tools. With older students, a handout with the points of the talk that includes the author's book title and ordering information works well.

> About one of every ten children attend private schools, most of them Christian.

Make sure the author also gives book ordering information with school discounts to the teacher for the school's future use to maximize the author's exposure at each speaking engagement. Some authors provide the school with pre-order forms for the children to pre-order the book at a special price, and then receive their book, signed by the author, on the day of the author's visit.

While a school may not purchase books immediately from an author who is speaking, remember that leaving marketing material and order forms can help secure future book sales especially when the author or publisher makes a follow-up contact. Make sure a thank you letter is sent to the teacher and the school administrators after each speaking engagement.

Educational Conferences

All teachers need ongoing certification credits. In order to accommodate this need, school associations host educational conferences for their school teachers and administrators. While some hold a national conference, many present regional conferences so that school employees do not have to travel far to acquire certification credits.

Educational conferences offer publishers many wonderful opportunities to present and promote books to teachers and school administrators. Most of the Christian school associations host annual conferences for their members. Many of these educational conferences feature exhibitor halls, where publishers can rent booth space to showcase products. Exhibiting is a great way to meet teachers and sell your books. Conferences also have sponsorship and advertising opportunities including advertising in the conference program, another great way to present your books to Christian educators.

Sarah Bolme

Publications

Communication is a major part of belonging to an association. All Christian school associations have some formal way that they communicate with their members schools on a regular basis. Most have a magazine or newsletter that is distributed to teachers and school administrators. These publications generally accept advertisements. Publishers that advertise their books in these periodicals know that they are getting direct exposure to hundreds of teachers.

School association publications include articles to help teachers and administrators increase their effectiveness. Good articles that give creative ideas on teaching are always welcome. Authors can submit articles to these publications. If published, the author's byline can include the author's books and website for ordering.

Many of the Christian school association publications also include a material review section. Having a Christian school teacher you know review a book and submit a review to their association's publication is a great way to get some free exposure for your book.

Direct Mail

Direct mailing promotional materials of your books to teachers and school administrators is another way to sell books to Christian schools. Most Christian school associations sell mailing lists of their member schools. Many list all their member schools online, so you could generate your own mailing list, although this requires an investment of time. Mailing list rental companies also rent lists of Christian and parochial school addresses. For example, Consolidated Mailing Services (www.educationlists.com) offers lists of private religious schools and/or Catholic schools.

Christian School Associations

The most effective way to reach the Christian school market is by using resources that Christian school associations provide. The major Christian school associations in the United States are listed here.

- **American Association of Christian Schools**
  www.aacs.org

- **Association of Christian Schools International**
  www.acsi.org

- **Association of Christian Teachers and Schools**
  www.actsschools.org

- **Association of Classical and Christian Schools**
  www.accsedu.org

- **Christian Schools International**
  www.csionline.org

- **Evangelical Lutheran Education Association**
  www.eleanational.org

- **Lutheran Missouri Synod Schools**
  www.lcms.org/schoolministry

- **National Association of Episcopal Schools**
  www.naes.org

- **National Catholic Education Association**
  www.ncea.org

- **National Christian School Association**
  http://nationalchristian.org

- **Seventh Day Adventist Schools**
  http://adventisteducation.org

- **Southern Baptist Association of Christian Schools**
  www.sbacs.org

Christian Colleges & Universities

In considering Christian schools, don't overlook Christian colleges and universities if this market is appropriate for your books. Christian colleges and seminaries generally have an on-campus bookstore and library for their students. Professors also choose textbooks and supplemental reading materials for the courses they teach their students. Many professors require students to read materials beyond the course textbooks and as such, are usually looking for new and creative books on topics of interest. Reaching professors is similar to selling to teachers.

Most of the Christian school associations include institutes of higher learning in their membership base. For these members, school associations generally host separate publications and conventions for their higher institutes of learning, providing publishers similar opportunities for marketing. There are also a number of associations for Christian institutes of higher education. Some of these list their members on their website or rent their membership list. A few have publications that publishers can advertise in. These associations include:

- **Association of Independent Christian Colleges and Seminaries**
  www.aiccs.org

- **Council for Christian Colleges and Universities**
  www.cccu.org

- **The Association for Biblical Higher Education**
  www.abhe.org

- **Transnational Association of Christian Colleges and Schools**
  www.tracs.org

- **Association of Catholic Colleges and Universities**
  www.accunet.org

- **The National Catholic College Admission Association**
  www.catholiccollegesonline.org

Bible Schools and Seminaries

Publishers with theological books should consider marketing to religious studies professors, libraries, and bookstores at seminaries and Bible schools. A few associations serve academicians in this market and provide resources for reaching this unique group.

- **American Academy of Religion (AAR)**
  AAR is the world's largest association of academics who research or teach topics related to religion. AAR is a "religious" organization rather

than a "Christian" organization in that the Academy does not endorse or reject any religious tradition or set of religious beliefs or practices. However, many Christian academic scholars are members of this academy. The AAR publishes four publications that accept advertisements. They also hold an annual meeting, which has opportunities for publishers to exhibit their books as well as advertise in the meeting's program. You can also rent a mailing list of their members.

American Academy of Religion
825 Houston Mill Rd. NE, Suite 300
Atlanta, GA 30329-4205
404-727-3049
www.aarweb.org

- **American Theological Library Association (ATLA)**
Membership in the ATLA is open to any person engaged in professional library or bibliographic work in theological or religious fields. The organization rents a mailing list of their member libraries, produces a quarterly newsletter that includes advertisements, and hosts an annual convention where publishers can exhibit their products or advertise in the convention program.

American Theological Library Association
300 South Wacker Drive, Suite 2100
Chicago, IL 60606-6701
888.665.ATLA
atla@atla.com
www.atla.com

- **Association of Theological Booksellers (ATB)**
ATB is an association of academic theological bookstores for seminaries and Bible schools. This organization produces a book catalog, *Theological Best Books*, twice yearly in the spring and fall. The spring edition features new and bestselling titles in pastoral ministry and spirituality while the fall edition features new and bestselling titles in theology, biblical studies, history, contemporary issues, and reference. These catalogs are shipped in bulk to seminary and theological center bookstores for distribution to students, seminarians, faculty, alumni, and other customers. The catalogs are also mailed to members of the American Academy of Religion and to subscribers of *The Journal of Pastoral Care*. ATB also rents mailing lists for seminary and Bible school academic bookstores.

Association of Theological Booksellers
PO Box 96
Sea Cliff, NY 11579
516-674-8603
Charles A. Roth, Executive Director
charles@rothadvertising.com
http://associationoftheologicalbooksellers.org

- **Association of Christian Librarians (ACL)**
  ACL serves evangelical librarians in institutes of higher education, mostly Christian colleges and universities. The organization publishes a journal twice a year and hosts an annual convention with opportunities to exhibit and advertise.
  Association of Christian Librarians
  PO Box 4
  Cedarville, OH 45314
  937-766-ACLL
  info@acl.org
  www.acl.org

Society of Bible Literature (SBL)
The Society of Biblical Literature is the oldest and largest international association of Bible scholars in the world. If your publication is Bible related, you can advertise with SBL. The Society publishes two annual journals that allow advertising. SBL also hosts an annual convention where publishers can exhibit or advertise their products. SBL also allows rental of their membership mailing list. Eblasts to their membership base can also be purchased to advertise your book.
Society of Biblical Literature
The Luce Center
825 Houston Mill Road
Atlanta, GA 30329
404-727-3100
sblexec@sbl-site.org
www.sbl-site.org

Christian Camps and Conference Centers

Christian camps and conference centers across the United States cater to thousands of Christians each year seeking spiritual renewal and respite. Every one of the fifty states in America is home to multiple Christian camps and conference centers. These centers present an avenue for publishers to promote their books to Christian consumers.

Christian camps and conference centers exist for spiritual renewal and growth. Books that fall into this category lend themselves to this market. Other books that also do well in this environment are books for children and teenagers, books on family matters, and gift books. However, local authors are always a draw, so a publisher with a book by an author local to a specific Christian camp or conference center might consider this avenue for book promotion as well.

Christian camps and conference centers present two main opportunities for book promotion.

Bookstores

Most Christian camps and conference centers support a bookstore on site. Many of these stores are extremely small and cater to the needs of the Christians who attend the center for spiritual retreats. Since these bookstores don't have much space, publishers should make direct contact with the individual responsible for overseeing the center's store to pitch their books. When contacting conference center bookstore managers, make sure to present some reasons why your particular book would be a good match for center attendees.

Typically camp and conference center gift store managers (most of whom are the camp director or one of the staff) do not attend Christian retail trade shows, nor are these stores CBA members. Camp and conference center gift stores tend to be small stores with very limited shelf space. Sales representatives, product catalogs, and word of mouth are how most of these stores decide on which products to stock.

Conference Center Rooms

Many conference centers include at least one upscale lodge with rooms that resemble hotel suites. These rooms often include a packet of promotional literature (brochures advertising products or nearby attractions) much like one would find at a hotel. Publishers with local authors or books with spiritual relevance to conference attendees can contact conference centers and inquire about the possibility of placing a brochure in these packets as a way to promote your books to conference attendees.

Sarah Bolme

Free books can spur sales. Consider giving free books to a conference center to get more sales. For example, request that the conference center place a free promotional copy of your book in each room of their facility (much like Gideon Bibles are placed in hotel rooms). Then place a note to the reader inside each book that would include information on how to order more copies of the book and how to book the author for a speaking engagement.

Locating Christian Camps and Conference Centers

Most Christian camps and conference centers belong to a camping association. These associations rent their mailing lists, provide some type of publication to their members (magazine, newsletter, or e-zine) that you can advertise in, and host annual conferences where you can exhibit your titles.

Here are some Christian camping associations to consider.

- **Christian Camp and Conference Association (CCCA)**
  This large association provides extensive programs, products, and services to autonomous Christian camps and conference centers nationwide. Their website contains the most extensive online database of Christian camps, conference centers, and retreat centers.

  The association produces a bimonthly magazine *Insight*, and hosts a national convention each year.
  www.ccca.org

- **Lutheran Outdoor Ministries**
  This ministry is for camps that serve the ELCA denomination. The ministry hosts an annual convention for their member camps and includes a listing of their camps on the website.
  www.lomnetwork.org

- **Mennonite Camping Association**
  This association is for camps belonging to Mennonite congregations and holding to those tenets of belief. This association produces a monthly newsletter and hosts a biennial conference.
  www.mennonitecamping.org

- **National Association of Christian Camps (NACC)**
  This organization has member camps across the United States. They produce a regular digital newsletter, *CAMPTALK*, for their members.
  www.naccamps.org

- **Presbyterian Church Camp and Conference Association (PCCCA)**
  PCCCA is the association for camps affiliated with the Presbyterian faith. The association hosts an annual conference and lists their member camps and conference centers on their website.
  www.pccca.net

- **Southern Baptist Camping Association**
  The Southern Baptist Church has numerous Christian camps across the country that are affiliated with their denomination. The association hosts an annual conference for their members.
  www.sbcamping.org

- **United Methodist Camp and Retreat Ministries**
  This association is for 200 camps serving the United Methodist Church. The organization hosts an annual gathering for their member camp leaders.
  http://umcrm.org

- **Young Life Camping**
  Young Life, an organization for middle and high school students, owns 23 camps across the country.
  www.younglife.org/camping

There are also a few websites that provide listings of Christian camp and conference centers. Two such websites are www.christianconferencecenters.com and www.mysummercamps.com.

Creative Marketing

Special sales can be secured with other organizations beyond Christian organizations. One author with a Christian book for kids about moving partnered with a local Christian realtor to buy her books in bulk as gifts to families who purchased a new house. Another author with a grief book secured bulk sales with a local Christian funeral home that was looking for a grief resource for their clientele. Yet another author with a book on how to declutter with a focus on blessing others with your abundance secured a bulk sale purchase with a local retirement home that used the books to give to retirees who were looking at downsizing.

Summary

Going beyond the traditional bookstore to partner with Christian organizations can help you sell more books. One positive aspect of partnering with Christian organizations is that they are often not as concerned as bookstores with the publication date of a book, so if your book is a couple years old, you can still use this venue to market and sell your book. Keep in mind that most partnerships don't happen on the first offer. If you practice patience and pleasant persistence, you will be able to find organizations to partner with.

Engage Christian Media

[My word] will not return to me empty, but will accomplish what I desire and achieve the purpose for which I sent it.
—Isaiah 55:11

> Marketing Fundamental:
> **Consumers trust the media they consume.**

We are a media society. Americans spend an average of 9.7 hours a day engaged with various types of media: news, radio, television, movies, and the Internet. Media coverage is one of the most effective ways to reach a large number of Christian consumers and generate interest in a book.

Whether you get your book reviewed in a newspaper or magazine, obtain an interview in the newspaper or on the radio or television, or advertise with a media outlet, most media coverage gives an author the opportunity to expose a large number of people to his or her book. There are a number of means authors can use to secure coverage with the media.

Christian Magazines

Literally hundreds of Christian magazines exist. A Christian magazine can be found for every category you can think of: children, teenagers, young adults, men, women, fathers, mothers, grandparents, senior adults, pastors, teachers, musicians, writers, nurses, counselors, businessmen and women, marriage, money management, prayer, etc. While many magazines are becoming digital online publications, print magazines still abound. Magazines provide a number of channels for you to market your books to consumers.

The best resource for a comprehensive list of Christian periodicals is *The Christian Writer's Market Guide*, now compiled by Jerry B. Jenkins. This resource is updated annually and provides a listing of current Christian magazines both print and digital.

The website www.christwriters.info/open-submissions.php hosts one large listing of Christian magazines. Two older sites have lists of Christian magazines, however, some of the publications listed are no longer operational. These two sites are www.faithstart.com/mags.html and www.findchristianmagazines.com.

Magazines provide three main avenues to expose Christian consumers to your books.

Advertisements

Advertisements drive the magazine industry. The bulk of a magazine's income comes from advertisements. If magazine advertisements were not effective, this income source for the magazine industry would have dried up long ago. However, it is important to remember that consumers generally need to see and hear about a product seven to twelve times before they will purchase. Therefore, when considering magazine advertisements, it is best to select carefully magazines that target the category of Christians your book is geared toward and budget for repeat advertisements in those publications.

Articles

Many Christian magazines' articles come from freelance writers' submissions. Editorial calendars and guidelines for article submissions generally can be found on a publication's website or requested from the magazine editor via email. The majority of magazines accept reprints (articles that have been printed in other publications) as long as the submission clearly states the article is a reprint and when and where it has been printed before.

Magazine articles are a powerful, free marketing tool for authors. Authors can submit articles based on the subject matter of their books or an excerpt from a book. Since most magazines accept secondary rights to material (meaning the material has been published elsewhere before), excerpts from books make great periodical articles. When these articles are accepted, the author's byline can list the title of the book, gaining publicity. Readers who are interested in the subject matter of the article will sometimes purchase the book to learn more.

This same technique can be used for fiction stories. Many magazines feature fiction pieces and will run a short story or an excerpt of a fiction book. An additional boon from article submissions for authors is that some publications provide payment for the articles they use.

Authors may need to get permission from their publisher prior to submitting book excerpts for publication. Some publishers' contracts specify that the publisher owns the book material while the book is in print. Generally, most publishers are willing to grant permission for authors to submit book excerpt articles as this helps with publicity.

Writing regular columns for magazines is another publicity option. Once you have published a few articles in a Christian magazine, you can approach that magazine's editor and suggest a regular column that you could write for the magazine. Columns are a good way to establish yourself as an expert in a subject, gather a loyal reader base, and generate ongoing exposure for your published books.

> Americans spend an average of 9.7 hours a day engaged with various types of media.

Book Reviews

A number of Christian magazines run reviews of books. However, most of these magazines do not have their own book reviewers. Rather, they accept book review articles from freelance writers. *The Christian Writer's Market Guide* indicates which publications print book reviews.

It is advantageous for a publisher to form a mutually beneficial relationship with a freelance writer. In such a relationship, the freelance writer agrees to review the publisher's books and submit book review articles on the books to various Christian magazines. The publisher benefits from the publicity and the freelance writer benefits from the income derived from the articles. One advantage of magazines is that a book does not need to be brand new for a publication to run a review. As long as the book is still relevant, the publication may decide to use the review.

There are a few online magazines devoted exclusively to covering Christian books. These magazines offer opportunities for advertising, book reviews, author interviews, and articles.

- **Book Fun Magazine**
  Book Fun Magazine is published monthly and covers all types of Christian books and authors. The magazine is produced by The Book Club Network, Inc.
  www.bookfunmagazine.com

- **Christian Fiction Online Magazine**
  This magazine is affiliated with the Christian Fiction Blog Alliance and is published monthly.
  www.christianfictiononlinemagazine.com

- **FamilyFiction and FamilyFiction Edge**
  These magazines are produced in alternating months. *FamilyFiction* covers Christian fiction books, while *FamilyFiction Edge* is devoted to suspense and speculative fiction.
  www.familyfiction.com

- **TWJ Magazine**
  This digital magazine seeks to connect readers with authors and publishers of Christian, inspirational, clean, and wholesome books.
  http://twjmag.com

Christian Newspapers

Over the past few years, the number of print newspapers has declined. Some have gone out of business, while others have ditched the print editions and become digital publications. There are still a number of Christian newspapers that are published and distributed throughout the United States. The majority of Christian newspapers are regionally distributed with each publication having its own feel and local appeal. Newspapers are definitely a medium not to be overlooked in a publisher's marketing plans.

Marketing Opportunities

Advertising in Christian newspapers is one means to accessing Christian consumers. Most Christian newspapers are offered to readers free of charge, thus these papers rely on advertisers to provide the revenue needed to sustain their operation.

Christian newspapers offer other marketing opportunities beyond advertising. Some newspapers run Christian product reviews, while others print announcements about local Christians and Christian organizations, and most include a calendar of Christian events for their area. Publishers can make use of these free opportunities in Christian newspapers either to have a product reviewed, submit a news release about an upcoming product, or place a notice in the paper's events calendar about an author's book signing at a local venue. Target Christian newspapers in both the publisher's and the author's communities for press releases on new books, especially if the newspaper can feature the author in an article. If an author is undertaking a book signing tour, make sure to send press releases for both articles and the events calendar to local Christian newspapers for every community in which your author will appear.

Associations

Christian newspapers are as plentiful and diverse as the Christian faith. While there is no central registry of Christian newspapers, there are a couple newspaper associations for Christian newspapers. Some of these associations list their members on their website while others provide a list of their members for a fee. Some host national conventions where publishers and authors can exhibit their books or advertise.

- **The Associated Church Press (ACP)**
  This is the oldest religious press association in North America. This association's members are publishers of ecumenical or interfaith publications whose majority readership is a Christian audience. They also host an annual convention.
  www.theacp.org

- **The Catholic Press Association (CPA)**
  CPA hosts a list of their member publications on their website. They also list national and regional Catholic newspapers that are members of CPA. CPA hosts an annual Catholic Media Conference. The association owns Catholic Advertising Network (CAN), an ad placement service for the Diocesan newspapers.
  www.catholicpress.org

- **Evangelical Press Association (EPA)**
  EPA exists to promote the cause of Evangelical Christianity and enhance the influence of Christian journalism. Their members

include publishers of both newspapers and periodicals. A listing of their members with links to each website is available on EPA's website. They also rent their member list for a fee. The association hosts an annual convention for their members.

www.evangelicalpress.org

Press Release Services

Press release services are a way to reach a large number of newspapers effectively. Press release services charge a fee to send a press release to their list of newspapers and journalists, although they provide no guarantee that the newspapers will print the information. However, should any newspapers decide to print an article, the featured book receives exposure to all the readers of the newspapers that print the story.

- **Christian Newswire (CN)**
  Christian Communication Network's Christian Newswire will send press releases to your specified target audience. Publishers and authors can choose from a list of 1,000 Christian radio, television, and print outlets nationwide or over 400 Catholic media outlets.
  www.christiannewswire.com

- **ChristianNewsToday.com Newswire Service**
  ChristianNewsToday.com will submit your press release to over 500 Christian media outlets.
  www.christiannewstoday.com/ChristianNewsToday.com_Press_Release_Service.html

- **Religion Press Release Services (RPRS)**
  RPRS distributes press releases to the subscribers of Religion News Service. Religion News Service subscribers include both secular and Christian newspapers.
  www.religionnews.com

Religion Coverage in General-Market Newspapers

One other newspaper resource worth mentioning is the religion section in local general market newspapers. Most newspapers have a religion section at least once a week. Many of these religion sections carry articles on local figures in the community. Sending a press release to the religion editor of the local newspaper where the author of your newest title lives can result in coverage of that author and the new book. It is important to slant your press release in a manner that will grab the attention of the religion editor and give her some material to consider that is of interest to the newspaper's reading audience.

Publishers and authors can search online for general market newspapers in your locale and then submit press releases to the religion reporters. Two websites that list newspapers across the United States by state are www.onlinenewspapers.com and http://newslink.org.

Another option is to utilize the advertising venues that the following organization provides to reach religion reporters:

- **Religion Newswriters Association (RNA)**
  This association is for print and broadcast reporters who cover religion in the general circulation news media. They have a few avenues available for publishers to reach their members with information on your latest books. RNA rents their mailing list of member reporters, they allow advertising on their site, they will send press releases to their members for a fee, and they host an annual conference where publishers can exhibit or advertise.
  www.rna.org

Services Linking Journalists and Experts

One good way to obtain news coverage is to meet the informational needs of journalists. Reporters frequently need experts to quote and when you have written a book, you become an expert on that book's subject.

A number of services allow journalists to send out requests for experts they need to interview for upcoming articles. You can sign up to receive these journalists requests and then respond to the ones for which you are qualified.

- **Help a Reporter**
  If you are serious about wanting to be quoted as an expert in your subject matter, then sign up for this free service provided by Peter Shankman. You can sign up as a provider of information on this website, and receive daily emails containing queries from reporters looking for sources on various topics. If you are qualified to comment on a topic and would like to be considered for an interview on the subject, you just reply directly to the journalist's email included in the query listing.
  www.helpareporter.com

- **PitchRate**
  Journalists and bloggers send in requests for information they are seeking. PitchRate sends a daily email alerting you to these requests. Qualified authors can respond directly to the journalists.
  www.pitchrate.com

- **ProfNet**
  An online community of nearly 14,000 professional communicators, ProfNet was created to connect reporters easily and quickly with expert sources. Reporters connect with experts either by sending an opportunity to the network or by searching the expert profiles. There is a fee to join this community.
  www.profnet.com

Publiseek
Publiseek is a daily email newsletter that provides you with journalists seeking news items and stories. You can sign up to receive this free daily email alert on the company's website.
  www.publiseek.com

Christian Radio and Television

According to Nielson, the average American over the age of two spends more than 34 hours a week watching live television. In essence, the average weekly TV viewing time has not changed much in recent years. Radio reaches an impressive 93% of all Americans over the age of 11. When you look at an entire broadcast day, radio reaches 59% of adults ages 25 to 54—second only to TV, which reaches around 80%. The average radio listener listens to about 14 hours of radio a week. Online radio (listening to radio over the Internet) is growing. Over 46% of Internet users ages 12 and up listen to online broadcasts at least once a week, making it one of the top web activities.

While it is not necessary to focus just on Christian radio and television stations to obtain publicity for a Christian book, doing so will allow you a greater chance of getting your book in front of your target audience. The number of Christian radio and television stations in the United States is astounding. The Barna Group reports that 46% of U.S. adults listen to a Christian radio broadcast in a typical month and that up to 63% of the Christian radio audience is female.

Some books lend themselves better to talk radio and television then others. Broader interest nonfiction adult Christian books on topics such as relationships, health, parenting, and the like are better candidates for radio and television exposure then many fiction or children's books. However, if a fiction or children's title has a unique angle that would be of interest to the general public, it could be a candidate for radio or television.

> The average radio listener listens to about 14 hours of radio a week.

Media Kit

Authors that are serious about securing interviews with the media must have a media kit. A media kit consists of an author photo, author biography, press release, book highlights sheet, testimonials, awards the book has won, list of interview questions, at least one video or audio recording of an interview, and contact information. Media kits used to be physical packages that were mailed to media personnel; they are now made available to media personnel online, usually on the author's website under a media tab.

If you have not had much media coverage, one good source for securing an interview that you can then purchase to include in your media kit on your website is the The Christian Authors Show (www.thechristianauthorsshow.com). This service will interview you for free and feature your interview on their website for a short period of time. They give you the option to purchase your interview and use it in your own promotional activities as you see fit.

Securing Interviews

Acquiring radio and television interviews is difficult work and having a fascinating topic and a great pitch letter improves your chances of catching a producer's attention.

The best way to access Christian radio and television stations is through a publicist. Producers want to know that they can trust a guest on their show to deliver what is promised. If an unknown author or publisher approaches a producer about booking a guest on their show, the producer has no guarantee that they will be interviewing someone who will be able to speak to their audience in an effective manner. This is where publicists can help. A good publicist has contacts with the major radio and television producers and already has a reputation in the industry. Producers know that they can trust the recommendation of the publicist. An up-to-date list of Christian publicists can be found in *The Christian Writer's Market Guide*.

Some publishers and authors don't want to pay the fees that publicists charge. They want to try to secure radio and television spots themselves due to a tight budget. If you fall into this category, take heart. It is possible to secure some media coverage without a publicist, but it will take time and effort on your part. Following are some resources for authors and publishers who don't want to engage a publicist to do the work for them.

Publicity Services

Publicity services vary depending on the amount of money you are willing to pay. One option is advertising in a publication that promotes radio and television media guests to producers.

- **Authors and Experts**
  This online listing service connects authors with media professionals. The service provides visibility to television and radio show hosts. Their fee for this service is very affordable.
  www.authorsandexperts.com

- **GuestFinder**
  GuestFinder is designed to make it easy for people who work in the media to find guests. This service provides an inexpensive way for talented professionals to announce their availability as media guests.
  www.guestfinder.com

- **National Religious Broadcasters (NRB)**
  The NRB is an association for Christian media personnel. The association publishes a convention magazine annually and a weekly e-newsletter. Publishers and authors seeking guest interviews can advertise in these publications. The NRB also hosts a national convention where publishers and authors can exhibit to draw the attention of broadcast producers.
  www.nrb.org

- *Radio and TV Interview Report*
  This magazine is produced twice a month and sent to over 4,000 radio and television producers who are seeking guests for their shows.
  www.rtir.com

- **Yearbook of Experts**
  This online directory is free for media personnel to browse when they need an expert for a news story or an interview.
  www.expertclick.com

Press Release Services

The cheapest option to attempt to gain the attention of news editors and radio and television show producers is to use a press release service (also called a news or media release service) to send your press release to targeted media and pray that your release will engage a producer's interest. The following press release services target Christian audiences for varying fees.

- **Christian Newswire (CN)**
  Christian Communication Network's Christian Newswire will send press releases to your specified target audience for a very reasonable fee. Publishers and authors can choose to tailor their press release distribution to a subgroup of media outlets such as Christian radio, television, and print outlets nationwide, Catholic media outlets, or target just one of the 50 states.
  www.christiannewswire.com

- **PR Newswire**
  PR Newswire will distribute your press release to thousands of media across the country.
  www.prnewswire.com

- **PRWeb**
  PRWeb will deliver your press release to every major search engine, national news sites, and 30,000 journalists and bloggers. While it does not target Christian media, many Christian authors can get publicity through general radio and television programs also.
  www.prweb.com

If you are on a shoestring budget, consider using the many free press release services on the Internet. Publishers and authors can submit press releases to one or all of these services to increase the possibility of reaching the media with their story. The old adage, "you get what you pay for," is true. These services provide no guarantees that anyone will actually print your story or call you for an interview once your press release is posted on the Internet.

These free services submit your press release content to search engines on the web. Then your press release is available for anyone searching for keywords listed in your release. Basically, these free press release services put your information out over the web via search engines, but they do not directly target news editors or radio and television producers.

Free press release services on the Internet include:

- www.24-7pressrelease.com
- www.1888pressrelease.com
- www.free-press-release.com
- www.newswiretoday.com
- www.prlog.org
- www.pr.com
- www.pagerelease.com
- www.prurgent.com
- www.przoom.com
- www.pressmethod.com
- http://pressreleasepoint.com
- http://freepressindex.com

Local Radio Stations

If you are new to public speaking and radio interviews, you can start with local Christian radio shows to acquire practice and experience with interviewing prior to taking on a national radio or television campaign. Interviews on local Christian radio stations can provide good publicity for your book. Local radio stations will be more likely to list you on their websites, announce ordering information for your book more frequently during an interview, and even ask you back for subsequent interviews, than the larger national radio shows and stations.

When seeking to secure an interview on a local radio station, make sure that your pitch letter includes the title of your book, your credentials, how your topic addresses current events, and why it is right for the show's audience. Include an accompanying list of 10 to 15 potential interview questions for the producer and copies of relevant reviews, endorsements, and newspaper articles you have secured on your book. It also helps to include a link to your website where there is some type of audio-visual recording of the author for the producer to preview. Some authors send a copy of their book with their pitch letter. However, don't just rely on your press releases and pitch letters to obtain interviews. Radio personnel are generally more auditory than visual. You will need to phone station producers after sending your queries to verbally request a guest interview. Producers need to feel secure that you will be entertaining and interesting enough to hold their audience's attention. Sometimes repeat phone calls are required to secure an interview.

Local Christian radio stations can easily be located by using a radio station finder on the Internet.

- **Radio-Locator**
  This comprehensive Internet radio station search engine features links to over 13,000 radio station web pages. Searches can be made by city or state as well as for radio station format such as religious, Christian contemporary, or gospel music.
  www.radio-locator.com

- **Catholic Radio Association**
  This association's website allows browsers to search for member Catholic radio stations by state in their Catholic Travel Radio Guide.
  www.catholicradioassociation.org

Christian Television Networks

There are a number of Christian television networks around the United States. Each hosts a variety of Christian shows some of which host guests. Most of the networks list their programming on their website where publishers and authors can search to find programs that feature guests. Some of the major Christian television networks include:

- **Catholic Radio and Television Network (CRTN)**
  www.crtn.org

- **Christian Broadcasting Network (CBN)**
  www.cbn.com

- **Christian Television Network (CTN)**
  www.ctnonline.com

- **Daystar Television Network**
  www.daystar.com

- **Eternal Word Television Network (EWTN)**
  www.ewtn.com

- **Sky Angel®**
  www.skyangel.com

- **Total Christian Television Ministries (TCT)**
  www.tct.tv

- **Trinity Broadcasting Network (TBN)**
  www.tbn.org

One website, www.christiantuner.com, lists 981 Internet Christian television and radio stations. This website hosts the most complete collection of live Christian radio and television stations, programs, on-demand programming, and podcasting links on the Internet.

Host Your Own Show on Local Cable TV

Most communities now host a local public access cable channel. These stations allow anyone to host a free half-hour show on a space available basis. Contact your local cable company for details on how to sign up to have your own show. The great benefit of doing this is that you can receive a copy of your show to use as demonstration video to show how you perform on television when seeking to be booked as a guest on another television program.

Summary

Media coverage, whether via Christian or secular media, gives your book exposure to potential new readers. While authors may not be able to expound on the spiritual aspects of their books during an interview with the secular media, don't dismiss this medium. Readers who engage with a book as a result of an author's secular media coverage can be led toward the Creator of the universe and a relationship with Him as a result.

Access Christian Consumers

> But encourage one another daily,
> as long as it is called Today, so that none of you
> may be hardened by sin's deceitfulness.
> —Hebrews 3:13

> Marketing Fundamental:
> **The more consumers see and hear about it,
> the more likely they are to purchase it.**

More books are being published today than ever before, and the number continues to increase. At the same time, the number of readers for those books isn't increasing at the same rate.

This begs the question: Are there enough readers for all the books? I believe there are.

Christian consumers abound in the United States. The most recent census figures place the population of the United States at 313.9 million people.

Surveys indicate that about 73% of these individuals identify themselves as Christian. That means that there are potentially over 229 million Christian consumers to whom you could market your books.

The Pew Research Center found that the number of individuals identifying themselves as "unaffiliated" in terms of religion is increasing. They also found that 6 million of these "unaffiliated" adults report that they are religious or spiritual in some way. Two-thirds of them say they believe in God (68%) and one in five (21%) say they pray every day. These "unaffiliated" individuals also represent a group of consumers that you could market your Christian books to.

Research shows that an unbeliever must have seven to twelve significant contacts with the Gospel message before they will become a Christian. This same principle holds true in marketing. Consumers generally need to be exposed to a new product seven to twelve times before they will purchase it. Familiarity is important. The more consumers see and hear about a product, the more likely they will eventually purchase the product. This theory holds true in marketing books to the Christian marketplace. Repeated exposure is essential. The more consumers see and hear about your books, the more likely they are to place orders for your titles.

In 2012, almost half of American adults read a book not required for work or school. Surveys indicate that Christian consumers tend to read more than the general public. This does not mean that it will be easy to get Christians to purchase your books. To succeed as a publisher in the Christian marketplace, you need to use every avenue you can to attract every Christian consumer who would benefit from or enjoy your books.

Author Book Signings

Authors who are willing to do book signings bring publishers an effective low-cost marketing tool. As an author, you do not need to be a known personality to have a successful book signing, nor do you need to embark on a national book signing tour to be effective. Start with where you live and schedule book signings at local Christian and general market bookstores in your town and surrounding communities. CBA, the Association for Christian Retail, encourages their member stores to host Christian author book signings as a way to increase store traffic. To find CBA member Christian bookstores in a given area, visit http://cba.know-where.com/cba.

Once you have scheduled a book signing, don't expect the bookstore to handle all the promotion of the event. Publishers or authors should provide the bookstore with posters announcing the book, author, and signing date.

Press releases should be sent to all local media regarding the upcoming book signing including the store location, date, and time of the event. If the Christian bookstore hosting the book signing has a list of local church congregations, use this list to send announcements (via snail mail or email) to local churches to include in their Sunday bulletins or on a community notice bulletin board. Publishers should list authors' appearances on their websites and authors should also list appearances on their individual websites. In addition, list your event on local calendars. Every community has them. You can find local calendars by searching online for events in the city your book signing will be held in.

At your book signing, be sure to have plenty of promotional materials. Bookmarks, postcards, and even pens or pencils can all help promote the book during and after the signing event.

Consider holding a contest during your book signing offering a prize to the winner. The prize offered for such a contest is best if it is something other than a book. Offering something related to the book's topic or theme works best. For example, if you have a cookbook or health book with recipes, you could offer an apron or special mixing bowl set. A contest does not need to be elaborate. You can simply have consumers leave a business card or paper with contact information in a bowl and let them know that the winner will be notified by telephone and will be able to pick up the prize at the bookstore following the book signing event.

> Consumers need to be exposed to a new product seven to twelve times.

Creativity can pay off at book signing events and draw attention from customers who may not normally stop. One example of this would be that for a book on Christianity and martial arts, the author could wear a martial arts uniform to the book signing.

When the book signing is finished, arrange to sign a few copies of the featured book for the bookstore and provide "Autographed by Author" stickers for these books. Also remember to follow up with a thank you note to the bookstore that hosted the book signing event.

Forming alliances with other authors can provide more ways to expose Christian consumers to your books. Alliances offer you opportunities for joint book signings. Hosting a multiple-author book signing, especially for new authors, can be a useful tool. A book signing featuring two, three, or four local authors draws more attention and brings in more Christian consumers than a single-author event. Alliances also provide other ways for you to cross-promote each others' books including website links and selling each others' titles at book signings.

Author Speaking Engagements

One surefire way to spread the word about a book is for the author to embark on a speaking campaign. Christian authors who pursue speaking engagements gain more attention for their books. Some authors have single-handedly propelled their books to bestseller status through traveling and speaking nationwide on a continual basis.

If you, like many authors, do not have the ability to travel and speak extensively due to other life commitments, don't overlook this important aspect of book marketing. Authors who are willing to do even a few speaking engagements will develop a loyal reader base and increase sales of their books.

Getting Started

A good place for authors to start speaking on their book's topic is through local bookstores and libraries. Many bookstores will host short seminars by authors for their patrons. Libraries do this also. Authors who take advantage of these opportunities can sell autographed copies of their books after these events and boost their sales.

Nonfiction authors have a built-in topic for speaking, but fiction and children's book authors can create opportunities for speaking, as well. For example, children's authors can volunteer to read their children's book at a bookstore or library during National Literacy Month (September). An author of a young adult fiction title can volunteer to lead a short seminar for teens on fiction writing at a local library. These ideas are just a few of the many opportunities that can be created for authors to schedule speaking engagements to promote their books.

While developing a public speaking ministry takes time, speaking publicly can pay off for those authors who undertake this aspect of their book marketing campaign. Initially, authors may need to speak for free and use each speaking engagement to sell books. However, once a speaking ministry is established, authors can begin to charge for their speaking services.

If an author has no previous speaking experience or is fearful of the idea of speaking in front of a group of people, then training in public speaking through reading books or taking classes on the subject can give the author the skills and courage needed to embark on a public speaking journey. One good place to gain know-how and confidence in public speaking is through joining a local Toastmasters club (www.toastmasters.org).

Securing Speaking Engagements

Speaking engagements must be cultivated and pursued. Opportunities only drop into the laps of those who have built the speaking side of their profession over time. Most new speakers will have to cultivate speaking engagements. All sorts of Christian events feature authors as speakers. Speakers are needed for events ranging from local women's and men's conferences to Christian education conferences, to youth or pastors conferences. Authors can seek out speaking engagements through identifying specific Christian events as potential speaking venues. If an author is a member of a certain church denomination, sometimes alerting the denominational headquarters of the author's availability to speak at various conferences for local churches can lead to speaking engagements.

When a conference has been identified as a potential speaking venue, the next step is for the author or publicist to contact the conference's organizers and present the author's bio and speaking topic for the conference planner's consideration. Keep in mind that most conferences book their speakers eight months to a year in advance of a conference.

Speakers Bureaus

Authors who are serious about embarking on a speaking ministry can take advantage of one of the many Christian speaker bureaus available on the Internet. These bureaus provide lists of Christian speakers that event planners can access to find speakers for their upcoming events. Most of these services charge a fee for a listing. Fees and requirements for listing vary depending on the services provided by the bureau.

- **Ambassador Speakers Bureau & Literary Agency**
  Ambassador is the oldest and leading Christian speakers bureau in the United States.
  www.ambassadorspeakers.com

- **AWSA**
  Advanced Writers and Speakers Association (AWSA) is an organization for Christian women who have written at least two books and speak to groups of 100 people at least three times per year. They provide a directory of their members on their website for organizations looking for speakers.
  www.awsa.com

- **Christian Meetings & Conventions Association (CMCA)**
  This organization is an association for Christian meeting planners. You can obtain a listing as a speaker for free. They do ask that you donate a portion of your proceeds back to the organization.
  www.christianmeeting.org

- **Christian Speaker Services**
  Christian Speaker Services represents speakers to event planners. This service takes a percentage of the speaker's fee for each event they book.
  www.christianspeakerservices.org

- **Christian Women in Media Association (CWIMA)**
  CWIMA is open to all Christian women actively working in media. They also host a speakers bureau for their members.
  www.cwima.org

- **CMG Booking**
  CMG Booking (Catholic Media Group) is the leading resource for anyone looking to book a Catholic speaker for their next event or conference. Over the last decade, CMG Booking has grown to become the nation's largest and most influential Catholic speaker's bureau, representing more Catholic speakers than any other organization. Catholic speakers can apply to be represented by CMG Booking.
  www.cmgbooking.com

- **Northwest Christian Speakers**
  Northwest Christian Speakers is a nondenominational, nonprofit bureau serving evangelical churches and Christian organizations with dynamic and gifted speakers. This bureau is for speakers in the Northwest region of the United States.
  http://www.nwspeakers.com/

- **SpeakerMatch**
  This is a secular service that matches speakers with speaking opportunities. For a fee, speakers can join this website. Organizations seeking speakers can search the site for qualified speakers or post their needs on the website. Then the qualified members can respond to the need and seek to secure the speaking opportunity.
  www.speakermatch.com

Market Your Books to Reading Groups

Reading groups (a.k.a. book clubs) have proliferated over the past decade thanks in part to Oprah and her book club, as well as the Internet. These reading groups should not be confused with the discount book clubs that allow readers to purchase discounted books at regular intervals. Reading groups are made up of individuals who read books and like to discuss what they have read with other people.

Reading groups generally choose what books to read based on the group members' nominations. The group votes on the nominated books and agrees on which books to read. Often word spreads from one reading group to another when one group really enjoys a book they have read and discussed. Thus one reading group can influence the reading choices of other groups. As a result, reading groups can be a great source of word-of-mouth advertising for publishers.

> The average reading group member reads 36 books a year.

The average reading group member reads 36 books each year, while the average reading American reads five books per year. Marketing to reading groups has become a hot trend in selling books and is a good way to generate both word-of-mouth recommendations and sales for books. Publishers must be creative in approaching marketing to reading groups. Authors can be a big help in this area through encouraging their friends and acquaintances who are in reading groups to have their book club consider the author's latest book; especially if the author is willing to make an appearance to the group.

You can tap into reading groups with the following marketing techniques.

Create Discussion Questions

Many publishers are now including discussion questions on the last pages of their books, both fiction and nonfiction. Printing discussion questions at the end of your next book allows a reading group to have a ready-made set of questions to use should your book be chosen as reading material. In addition to printing discussion questions on the back pages of your next book, post discussion questions (called a reading group guide) on your website.

Encourage your authors to be available for phone chats and personal visits to reading groups. Many reading groups enjoy talking with the author of a book they have read and are discussing. Use your service as an author willing to chat with reading groups to promote your book to reading clubs. Post availability on your website and on online directory sites for reading groups. Some reading group directory sites allow publishers or authors to promote an author's availability and book to reading groups; usually for a fee.

— Sarah Bolme —

Advertise on Book Club Sites

There are a few websites on the Internet that provide services to book clubs. These sites provide reading group guides, author chats, and information about new books to reading groups around the world. Publishers and authors can use these websites to advertise their new books to reading groups. Following are five of the larger book club sites on the Internet.

- **The Book Club Network Inc.**
  The Book Club Network is an online book club for Christian reading groups around the world. Members (anyone can join) can nominate a book for the Book Club Book of the Month. Members then vote each month on the Book of the Month. Publishers and authors can advertise their books to book clubs in The Book Club Network's monthly digital magazine, *Book Fun Magazine*.
  www.bookfun.org

- **Reader's Circle**
  With over 90,000 registered reading groups, Reader's Circle is the leading book club networking site on the Internet. Authors can advertise that they are available for half-hour book chats by phone with reading groups. Listings for phone chats are easy to place and run for one-month on the home page. Afterwards, they are added to the author phone chat database for a full year.
  www.readerscircle.org

- **Reading Group Guides**
  Reading Group Guides caters largely to secular reading groups. Publishers can submit reading guides to this site. The site charges a fee of $150 to list your reading group guide. The guidelines for submitting a reading guide can be found on the website. This service also offers other opportunities for publishers and authors to advertise books to their list of over 10,000 registered reading groups.
  www.readinggroupguides.com

- **Book Movement**
  Another largely secular site, this online book club service hosts over 32,000 registered book clubs. Publishers and authors can advertise their books and host book giveaways and author chats through this service—all for a fee.
  www.bookmovement.com

- **BookShout!**
  While BookShout! is not a book club, it does have "reading circles." BookShout! is more of a social reading site. This social site allow readers to create reading circles where users can hold virtual book discussions around a particular ebook. BookShout! also allows authors to create a following, build a community around a book, and interact with readers.
  www.bookshout.com

Promote Your Books at Local Book Festivals

One great venue to promote books locally is through book festivals. Many towns host annual book or literary festivals. Some are one-day events while others span a week. These festivals are generally hosted by libraries, reading groups, nonprofit organizations, and even author or publisher associations. Book festivals offer some great opportunities to promote your books.

Sell Your Books

Book festivals feature publishers, authors, and bookstores selling books. Since book lovers attend book festivals, many opportunities for exposing readers to your books and selling your books are present at a book festival. Some festivals allow local authors to set up a table to sell books for free while others charge a fee to rent a table to sell books. If you set up shop at a local book festival make sure that you take plenty of promotional materials to hand out to increase your exposure and future sales.

Give a Literary Reading

Local book festivals love to feature local authors. Festivals offer book readings and other author presentations to draw attendees. Many festivals actively seek local authors to participate. Authors and publishers can contact a festival's organizing committee to let them know of an author's availability to participate.

Volunteer to Host a Writing Workshop

Book festival organizers are always looking for additional draws to entice the public to attend their book festival. As an author, you can volunteer to teach a short writing workshop on your area of expertise. If you write fiction for teens, volunteer to host a fiction writing workshop for teenagers.

Sarah Bolme

Likewise, if you write nonfiction, volunteer your service for hosting a workshop for beginning writers. If you are a children's book illustrator, consider presenting a quick art lesson or art project for children. Again, contacting the festival's organizing committee to let them know of your interest and availability will allow you to take optimal advantage of this great publicity opportunity.

Finding Local Book Festivals

Authors and publishers can use the Internet to search for local book festivals. Generally, typing "book festival" and your locale into a search engine will yield a number of results.

There are two great websites for finding local book festivals.

- **The Library of Congress (LOC)**
  The Library of Congress has an extensive listing of book festivals and fairs around the country. Each of the festivals listed on the LOC is either free to the public or only charges a nominal fee for attendees, making these festivals the best bet for lesser-known local authors to be able to participate in a manner that brings optimal exposure.
  www.read.gov/resources

- **Festivals.com**
  This website specializes in listing festivals of every flavor. However, you can use the site's search engine to search for festivals by state or by keyword (such as "books") to find local book festivals. The site also offers advertising opportunities at the festivals listed on their site.
  www.festivals.com

While most book festivals are secular affairs with sparse Christian representation, they do offer an inexpensive (and sometimes free) avenue for promoting your books. As Christians we are called to be the salt and light of this world, so let your light shine wherever your books take you!

Public Libraries

While public libraries are not Christian institutions, large numbers of Christians frequent public libraries and borrow books. As a result, many libraries feature Christian titles for their patrons. Public libraries across the country purchase large numbers of books. Placing your title in front of public library book buyers can result in book sales.

For libraries to purchase them, your books should contain a Library of Congress Control Number (LCCN) and should be listed with a library jobber (a wholesaler that librarians purchase from). Three major library jobbers are:

- **Baker & Taylor**
  www.btol.com

- **Brodart**
  www.brodartbooks.com

- **Midwest Library Services**
  www.midwestls.com

There are a number of good ways to market your books to public libraries.

Advertisements in Library Journals

The foremost publications libraries use to determine which books to buy are *Booklist*, *Library Journal*, *Publishers Weekly*, and *ForeWord Reviews* (see chapter 5). Besides striving to have your book reviewed in one of these publications, which will virtually guarantee sales of your book to libraries, you can place advertisements in these periodicals as another venue for bringing your titles before library book buyers.

Direct Mail

You can rent a public library mailing list such as one that is offered by the American Library Association (ALA) that features nearly 40,000 of their members (http://www.ala.org/aboutala/contactus/marketing/mail_list_rental) and send your brochure or catalog directly to libraries. Another option is to participate in an eblast program to libraries such as the one that BookMarketingBlast (www.bookmarketingblast.com) offers.

Library Association Meetings

The most cost-effective way to exhibit your titles at national and state library association meetings is to use an exhibit service. One such service is Combined Book Exhibit (www.combinedbook.com). This company provides book representation at the major library association meetings for a reasonable fee.

Friends of the Library Groups

Friends of the Library groups exist to support local public libraries. Most public libraries have such a group. These groups raise financial and community support for a library. Many of these groups publish newsletters that are made available to library patrons, and they schedule author speaking engagements for their local library. As an author, you can submit articles for these newsletters and alert your local Friends of the Library group of your willingness to be a featured speaker at a library. To contact your local Friends of the Library group, ask your local library for the contact information. A comprehensive list of public libraries listed by state can be found on the web at www.publiclibraries.com.

The Association of Library Trustees, Advocates, Friends and Foundations (www.ala.org/united) is an organization that supports local chapters of Friends of Libraries. They sponsor Authors for Libraries (http://authorsforlibraries.org) where authors can join and be listed for libraries seeking local authors for events.

Foreign Rights

Foreign rights are a great way to enlarge the audience for your books. Foreign rights contracts allow publishers in other countries secure the right to translate and sell your book in their language. Tens of thousands of books are translated into another language each year.

Roughly 60% of all translations around the world are books originally written in English. There is a demand by foreign publishers for English-language books they can translate and sell in their own countries. As a result, selling foreign rights for your books is a viable revenue stream to pursue.

Foreign rights are best obtained through partnering with a foreign rights agent. Be sure to find a reputable one to work with. Keep in mind that you should not have to pay a foreign rights agent in advance to find language-rights contracts for your books. Much like literary agents, most reputable foreign rights agents get paid on commission—when they sell the language rights for your book.

Creative Marketing

The average American citizen is exposed to over 3,000 advertising messages a day. It is extremely difficult to grab and catch consumers' attention in the midst of that many messages. In marketing, it is the out-of-the-box, creative ideas that are often the most effective in gaining attention. The number of ways to place your books in front of Christian consumers and generate sales is endless. Thinking outside the box can be useful in finding effective ways to market your titles.

Cause Marketing

Publishers and authors can use cause marketing to increase book sales. Cause marketing involves giving a portion of the proceeds of each book sale to a charity. Consumers want to know that businesses are helping to make the world a better place, not just getting rich from selling products.

Americans are exposed to over 3,000 advertising messages a day.

Christian consumers are no exception. Studies show that consumers like to purchase products when they know that a portion of the sale is going to help improve our world. The Cause Marketing Forum reports that 93% of consumers want to know what companies are doing to make the world a better place and that 34% promote cause-release brands.

Many publishers post on their website that they give a portion of their proceeds to charity. This is not the same as cause marketing. Cause marketing allows a customer to know exactly how much of their money is going to a specific cause or charity. In other words, let the customer know that one dollar (or however much you are willing to give) for every book sold will be given to the charity.

The key to a successful cause marketing campaign is fit. The cause you are donating to should fit the theme of your book. This makes it a powerful tug in the heart of the consumer. Remember that, just like selling anything, marketing must be done to get the word out to your audience that you are donating a portion of each sale to the cause you have picked. Advertise your specific commitment on the book's back cover, on your website, in all your marketing materials for the book, and on your social media sites. After all, addressing the desires of social-minded consumers gives readers one more reason to buy your books, which means more sales.

Hold a Contest

One Christian author offered a half-carat sapphire to generate traffic to her website and promote her book, a novel about a gemologist. Another author featured a riddle in her book and offered a cash prize to the first five readers who solved the riddle. One publisher sponsored a contest on one of their fiction author's books. They invited fans to publicize the author's new book and submit the results of their publicity efforts via email to the publisher. The winner received an expense-paid trip to a women's conference to hear the author speak and had a character named after her in the author's next book.

Yet another publisher hosted a fiction contest for the English classes in the high schools in his area. He contacted the English teachers for each school and let them know about the contest as well as provided literature on the contest for each class. This gentleman then published the winning fiction story and involved the teenage author in the publishing and marketing process so the young winning author could learn about book publishing. You can bet the school purchased some of those books. The contest was well received by the schools and so successful the first year, that this publisher has continued the contest each year. As a publisher of books that high schools might purchase, this gentleman was savvy in making his name and publishing company known to local schools. He also garnered a lot of local press coverage for his contest and the winning piece that became a book.

Use Swag

Humans love free stuff. We flock to freebies—sometimes referred to as swag. Swag is slang for plunder—getting stuff free. It has been retrofitted to be an acronym for "stuff we all get." You can use swag to draw attention to your books. Notepads, pens, mints, magnets, chip clips, key chains, and bookmarks are all great examples of swag. These novelty items with a book title or website printed on them make great marketing tools.

Publishers and authors can use swag at book promotion events such as speaking engagements and book signings to draw potential customers. A customer is more likely to approach a sales table if there is something free being offered on the table. The best freebies are useful items, not trinkets that will collect dust. A useful item that ties into the theme of a book has the most impact. One author with a book on time management gave away hourglass egg timers with his book title and website printed on each one.

The cost for imprinted promotional novelties can be as cheap as a few nickels to as expensive as over $100 per item. The following companies provide affordable items that can be purchased in bulk to be used as swag.

- **Business Boosters**
    www.atlaspen.com

- **Crestline**
    www.crestline.com

- **4 Imprint**
    www.4imprint.com

- **Oriental Trading**
  www.orientaltrading.com

Local Craft Fairs

Authors can sell books at local craft fairs. Communities as well as churches hold these events. When attempting to peddle books at a craft fair, be sure to have something to catch people's attention, and a way to help them know why to buy your book. Promoting a book as a good gift idea is a great way to capitalize on your presence at a craft fair, especially if it is around a holiday. One self-published author (with a children's book about how to deal with the arrival of a new sibling) advertised her book as a great baby shower gift or christening gift. Often older children feel left out when the fuss is over the new baby. Promoting her book in this creative way gave the author a great marketing edge at the craft fair.

Bundling

Have you ever noticed that few coffee shops just sell coffee? They usually offer pastries to go along with your coffee. Likewise, few sweet shops just offer sweets. They also sell drinks to help quench the thirst sweets produce. Often, these shops offer a deal, like "Buy a cupcake and get your drink for half price." This is called product bundling. Product bundling is a marketing strategy that offers several products for sale as one combined product. This bundle of products is sometimes referred to as a package deal.

Stores are not the only sellers that can benefit from bundling. Authors and publishers can too.

Consider offering a creative bundling package for your books. Offer products that tie into a book's theme to entice sales. For example, if you have a book that has a gardening or flower theme, offer a couple of flower seed packets with every purchase of a print book. This type of bundling places your book into the gift category, enticing more consumers to buy. Now, the gift giver is not just giving a book, but seeds for their gardening gift recipient.

Bundling with a tie-in product theme requires a little creativity. Who is the book geared to? What type of products does this audience like that might push them into buying your book?

Many authors and publishers don't consider tie-in bundling because of the expense. Purchasing T-shirts in quantity can be pricey, requiring funds up front and risking a loss if the sales strategy ends up not working. In addition, many authors have their hands full just with producing and marketing books. They don't have the time to learn the process of producing a stuffed animal to go with their children's book.

This is where networking can be helpful. If you want to offer a piece of jewelry with a book, partner with someone who has a business making jewelry. The two of you can develop a piece or line of jewelry specifically for your book. This way the jewelry does not need to be mass produced, but manufactured a few at a time as sales come in. Partnering with another small business owner to create a bundle can also increase your marketing reach. With such a partnership, two of you will be offering the bundle to your customer base, doubling your marketing reach.

> In 2012, almost half of American adults read a book not required for work or school.

Bookcrossing

Bookcrossing is the practice of leaving a book in a public place to be picked up and read by others, who then do likewise. At www.bookcrossing.com, you can register a book and then set the book free to travel the world and find new readers. Authors and publishers can use Bookcrossing to draw attention to their books.

Here is how it works. First become a member of Bookcrossing (it's free). Then pick a book you have written or published. Register the book on the website and generate a Bookcrossing ID for the book. Write the Bookcrossing ID inside the cover of the book and add the Bookcrossing information including the website so the reader will know what to do. Then release the book into the world. You can leave the book anywhere someone might pick it up and not consider it trash or a security risk. The book could be left at a coffee shop, on a church pew, in a newspaper box for free papers, on a park bench, in a gym locker room, or a doctor's office waiting room. The possibilities are endless. Then wait for an email notification from Bookcrossing that someone has made a journal entry on the book you released.

Once a book is picked up and the reader journals it into the Bookcrossing website, publishers can track where the book goes. If the book is actively moving, you could use this activity to promote the book on your website or blog showing where the book has traveled and what readers are saying. One word of caution, this is not guaranteed to work. Currently only a minority of books (about 20 to 25 percent) that have Bookcrossing ID numbers have been entered into the website by a reader who picked the book up.

Even if the book does not get picked up right away, Bookcrossing offers a cheap potential publicity stunt. For the price of a book or two, you could have a great story.

— *Sarah Bolme* —

Books take time to travel. Maybe years from now someone halfway around the world may make a journal entry on one of your books. The bottom line is if you publish books to promote the gospel and change lives, just imagine the possibilities of where God could take your book and whose lives could be touched.

Summary

King Solomon declared, "Of making many books there is no end, and much study wearies the body" (Ecclesiastes 12:12). This can also be said of marketing. Of marketing ideas there is no end, and too many overwhelm an author or publisher. There are more marketing ideas than can fit into one book. Let the ideas here help you develop an effective plan for your books.

Sarah Bolme

13

Harness the Internet

*A town built on a hill cannot be hidden.
Neither do people light a lamp and put it under a bowl.*
—Matthew 5:14–15

> Marketing Fundamental:
> **The Internet is your optimal marketing tool.**

The Internet has become an integral part of American life. Only 15% of adults in the United States choose not to use the Internet, leaving 85% that do use it. In today's market, the Internet cannot be ignored. As Internet connectivity has risen, the web has become an essential marketing tool for every publisher and author to reach their target audience. Publishers and authors must learn to harness the Internet to promote and sell books successfully.

Books continue to be one of the most popular items purchased on the Internet. In 2012, 43.8% of books bought by consumers were purchased online, while only 31.6% of books were purchased in large retail chains, independent bookstores, other mass merchandisers, and supermarkets. Today, about one in six new books are discovered online in some form.

Create a Website

Every publisher should have a website. In today's marketplace, if you do not have a website, your business does not exist. At a minimum, every author should have a website, but a website for every book you publish is also a good marketing tool. A survey conducted by Verso Digital found that an overwhelming 88% of respondents said that when it came to online book purchases search engine results and author websites and blogs were the most effective marketing tools in making them aware of a book. A web presence is an essential element of a marketing plan for books. You need a web presence just to begin to compete.

> Every sale has five basic obstacles: no need, no money, no hurry, no desire, no trust.

Websites are not expensive. There are a number of services online that allow you to create and maintain a website for free or for very low fees. However, with growing e-commerce, merely having a website is not enough. As Internet use continues to grow, your business website must not only attract visitors, it must also be "convincing" so that visitors who find your website will actually purchase your products.

Zig Ziglar, a master salesman and motivational speaker, once said, "Every sale has five basic obstacles: no need, no money, no hurry, no desire, no trust." A well-crafted website can help you overcome some of these obstacles. With your website, you can help create a need and a desire in the customer by showing them how your book meets a need in their life, help them trust that you have an excellent product to meet their need, and give them a reason to hurry by offering a limited-time special.

The majority of visitors to any given website will never purchase a product or service. It's true across the Internet. Only 6 out of every 100 visitors actually purchase something on Amazon.com. The other 94 visitors are just browsing. This is why having convincing and engaging website material can make a difference in converting website visitors to buyers.

Think of your website as a billboard. The vast majority of Internet users scan material rather than read word-for-word. Therefore, making the most of a few words works better than having lots of text. People are short on time. When they visit your website, they want the facts and want them fast.

Time is precious to people. They don't want to waste it. Your website page load speed affects everything from search engine ranking to revenue.

Amazon.com has found that it increased revenue by 1% for every 100 milliseconds of improvement in the page load speeds of its webpages. Shopzilla.com cut its average page load time from 6 seconds to 1.2 seconds and saw a 25% increase in page views and a 12% increase in revenue. The faster your site load time is, the higher your search engine ranking will be.

Visitors view more pages on websites that load quickly. So, if you want people to stay on your website, make sure your website loads quickly. You can check how fast your website loads using a couple of online tools. Two websites that offer instant free analyzing tools are http://tools.pingdom.com and www.websiteoptimization.com/services/analyze.

Studies show that the average user used to spend seven seconds on a website before deciding to leave or stay. Now, that time has shrunk to less than half a second. That is a very short time for your webpage to convince someone to stay. Convincing and engaging website material should include the following elements:

The WIIFM Factor

The WIIFM (What's In It For Me) factor tells people how your book meets a need in their life. Why should they stay on your website or look at your books? What is in it for them? Be clear about this on your site.

Eye Catching Images

Visitors to your website search for fixed points or anchors to guide them through the content of the page. In other words, if a website does not have an easy, visually-appealing way for visitors to find the information they are looking for quickly, they will leave.

The first place Internet surfers' eyes go to when they land on a website is the upper left quadrant of a site. That's where your primary message should be placed. This is called your headline. A headline should be seven to ten words and should sum up what it is you do for your customers (e.g., "Books to Help You Grow Spiritually"). The second place Internet surfers' eyes go is to the center of your page. This place should contain your call to action. Your call to action can be an offer of reading a few chapters free or it can be a special deal (e.g., "Buy the physical book and get the ebook free today"). These two primary places are significant in engaging visitors on your site. You have a very short time to let your website visitors know what you have to offer them.

Keep your website clean, but not too plain. Use a few colorful and eye catching images on your website, but not so many images that your webpage load speed is slow. If your site is too busy, it detracts from its appeal and usability, limiting its effectiveness. On the other hand, if your website is too plain and looks like it was designed 10 years ago and hasn't been updated, you also risk losing website visitors and potential customers. It is extremely important that the navigation of a website makes it easy for visitors to find what they came for in a few clicks.

A Call to Action

A clear message and fresh content are important to your website, but a call to action is required to engage website visitors and help you grow an ongoing marketing list. Whether you want your website visitors to purchase your books today or whether you want to collect their email addresses for future engagement, a call to action on your website is needed to draw your visitor in.

If you want your website visitors to purchase right away, then offer a special for your call to action. This special can be free shipping, a "buy one get one" deal, or a discount. If your purpose in your call to action is to collect email addresses to engage people over time, then offer something in exchange for their email address. This can be giving them a few sample chapters to read, asking them to sign up to receive notices of new book releases, asking them to take a survey, or offering a giveaway that requires visitors to give their email address to be entered into the drawing.

Contact Information

Many small business web pages lack specific contact information other than an email address. Placing specific contact information (address and phone number) increases visitors' security that your business is "real." It also increases visitors' confidence that, if they encounter a problem in ordering, they will be able to speak with a person about the problem.

Testimonials

Your website should provide testimonials from satisfied customers and reviews from known industry book reviewers. Testimonials increase your website visitors' confidence that a book is worth the money they will invest in it. However, be sure to obtain permission from your sources prior to posting their names and quotes on your website.

Associations, Affiliations, and Awards

Membership in a recognized industry association, along with the display of that association's logo on your website, can be convincing to visitors because it adds legitimacy and validates your business. Posting awards that you have received for your books increases the odds that visitors will purchase a book.

A Freebie

Freebies can take a number of forms and serve the purpose of inviting visitors to connect with your material. A sneak preview of a book through posting a chapter or two from that book is one type of freebie. This type of freebie is comparable to Amazon.com's Search Inside™ program, which was developed to encourage customers to purchase books. Another type of freebie is a website posting of an article on a related topic to a book's theme made available for a visitor to read or download. Freebies can also be a product that you throw in for free when a customer purchases your book. Your free product can be as small as a bookmark or as large as an additional book (maybe a title you are phasing out and want to clear out of your back stock).

Freebies can also help you begin to collect email addresses to begin your own email list for marketing purposes. Simply provide a freebie in exchange for the person's name and email address.

Advertise Online

Once you have developed a convincing website, your next challenge is to draw visitors to your website to view your material. There are a number of avenues available online to help draw traffic to your website as well as to market your books to potential purchasers.

One good way to draw traffic to your website or book is through online advertising. This is paid advertising on the Internet. A recent survey asked people why they buy the particular books they do. The responses were: author reputation (52%), personal recommendation (49%), price (45%), book reviews (37%), cover/blurb (22%), and advertising both print and online (14%). This survey indicates that advertising does help sell books. Online advertising takes many forms including search engine results, banner ads, and pop-up and pop-under ads.

AdWords Campaigns

AdWords campaigns are search engine placements based on words provided to a search engine. These advertisers get their websites listed first on the search engine results for the words they supply. The advertiser then pays based on the number of Internet users who click on their listing and are redirected to their website. Advertisers do not actually pay for the listing, only when the listing is clicked on; this is called pay-per-click.

Three popular search engine result ad placement services are:

- **Google™ AdWords**
  http://adwords.google.com

- **Yahoo! Advertising**
  http://searchmarketing.yahoo.com

- **Bing Ads**
  https://bingads.microsoft.com

Banner Ads

Banner ads are much like traditional advertisements. They are advertisements placed on websites notifying people of a product or service and why they should purchase it. Banner ads contain a link to the advertiser's website so that when a viewer clicks on the banner ad they are taken to the website where the product or service can be purchased. Banner ads can be static or animated. They can be a simple JPEG image or a more complex multimedia object (animation and sound) using technologies such as Shockwave or Flash. There are services online that help you create animated banner ads. These services include www.addesigner.com or www.bannermakerpro.com.

Publishers and authors can target specific websites to place banner ads on. Many websites accept banner advertisements for a monthly fee. The fee depends on how much traffic the site generates. There are also banner ad agencies that target your specified demographic via appropriate websites and charge either a monthly or a pay-per-click fee. Banner ad agencies include www.advertise.com and www.adready.com.

Pop-up or Pop-under Ads

A pop-up ad is where a new window opens in front of the current Internet page being viewed and displays an advertisement or website. A pop-under ad is similar to the pop-up ad except the window is loaded behind the current Internet page so that the user only sees it when they close the active window.

Pop-up and pop-under ads generally cost the advertiser per view. Again, ad services online specialize in helping advertisers develop and target these type of ads on the Internet. Two such services are www.infinityads.com and www.adonnetwork.com.

Advertise on Blogs

Posting advertisements on blogs whose subjects are related to your books' topics or that reach the demographic you are targeting can be a great marketing strategy. To find blogs that post advertisements, you can conduct your own blog search using lists of Christian blog aggregators at sites such as www.blogs4god.com or http://faithfulbloggers.com.

Once you identify some potential blogs, you can then approach each blog site individually with your request to advertise. An easier method is to use an existing blog ad service such as www.blogsvertise.com or http://beaconads.com. Blog ad services break blogs down by category (e.g., evangelical, homeschooling, parenting, etc.) with a listing of blogs that are currently accepting ads. You indicate which blogs you want to advertise on and the service then facilitates the deal for you.

Christian Advertising Networks

There are a number of general advertising services (some listed above) on the Internet. These services are legitimate and will help you acquire attention for your books. However, since many do not cater to Christian products, the vast majority of the sites available may not reach your target Christian audience. The best bet in reaching your target audience is to advertise on Christian sites.

There are a few Christian advertising networks online that can help you do just that. These include:

- **Beacon**
  http://beaconads.com

- **FaithAdNet**
  www.faithadnet.com

- **GodClick**
  www.godclick.com

- **Cross+Ads**
  www.crossads.net

Affiliate Programs

Affiliate programs are a referral-based marketing strategy designed to drive traffic to your website and increase your online sales. With this type of advertising, you only pay the website hosting your advertisement when a customer connects to your website through the advertisement and makes a purchase. Generally this fee is a commission (a percentage of the sale).

Affiliate marketing is a $4 billion industry. This strategy continues to grow and become an integral part of Internet marketing and sales. Marketing through affiliate programs is a great low-cost way to advertise. In a pay-per-sale model (PPS), you do not pay for banner placement or advertising, you only pay for results. If an affiliate drives visitors to your site, but these visitors don't purchase, you don't owe the affiliate any money.

> Friday is the best day of the work week to conduct email marketing.

If you are selling your books directly from your website and wish to develop your own affiliate program to increase website traffic and book sales, it is possible to develop an effective affiliate program. The cost to you is the time it takes to find and recruit websites whose visitors would most likely be interested in your books. For example, if you sell Bible-study materials, you could search for those websites that cater to individuals interested in learning more about the Bible and approach these websites to encourage them to become an affiliate for your products.

When establishing your own affiliate program, tracking technology is required to track which sites your sales come from. You can establish your own affiliate program, purchase tracking software, and pay commissions directly to your affiliates; or you can use an existing affiliate service that tracks the commissions for you such as www.clickbank.com and www.payloadz.com.

Affiliate programs offer a great online marketing tool that is very cost-effective since payment is only made when a sale occurs. This type of marketing increases both traffic to your website and sales of your books.

Conduct Email Campaigns

An email marketing campaign is similar to a direct snail-mail campaign except that the marketing is done via email addresses over the Internet rather than physical addresses through the post office. Email campaigns are more cost effective than direct mail campaigns. Email campaigns increase their effectiveness when repeat messages are used (email messages are sent repeatedly over a period of time). Research indicates that Friday is the best day of the work week to conduct an email marketing campaign. While more than a third of email messages are opened on any given day, Friday consistently outperforms the other days for the ratio of messages read.

Two options are available for securing email addresses to run email campaigns. One is to collect your own list of emails through offering a freebie on your website and requiring the people give you their email to get the freebie. The other way is to rent an email list (similar to renting a postal mail list) from companies that offer targeted email marketing services. A few such companies include:

- **Catholic Online**
    www.catholic.org

- **TriMedia**
    www.trimediaonline.com

- **ExactTarget**
    www.exacttarget.com

To conduct your own email marketing campaign with the email addresses you collect requires the use of an email service such as www.constantcontact.com or www.mailchimp.com. These services allow you to send email messages out in bulk format.

Create Book Videos

As technology advances, so must the marketing tools for gaining consumers' interest in books. As media becomes more interactive, consumers are responding better to promotional materials that touch multiple senses. In any given day, 89 million people in the United States watch 1.2 billion online videos. Studies have found that retail site visitors who view video stay two minutes longer on average and are 64% more likely to make a purchase than other site visitors.

Videos are effective in promoting books. Book videos, also known as book previews, are a great tool for promoting books on the Internet. Static book promotions only reach the eyes, while book videos connect with multiple senses. Book videos can hook people into wanting to read the book—much like movie trailers hook viewers into wanting to see the whole movie. These creative mini-films allow consumers to view a series of pictures with narration and music, creating a glimpse into a book. They remind the viewer that books are movies of the mind.

The cost to produce a professional book video can be fairly expensive. A few professional producers of book previews include:

- **Trailer to the Stars**
  www.trailertothestars.com

- **Circle of Seven Productions**
  www.cosproductions.com

- **Expanded Books™**
  www.expandedbooks.com

> Visitors who view a video stay two minutes longer and are 64% more likely to make a purchase.

Many authors and publishers are using Windows Movie Maker to create their own book videos in a cost-effective fashion. However, this method can be tricky because if the video ends up looking or sounding homemade, viewers may shy away from the book, assuming that it will not have much quality either. There are a few services on the Internet that allow you to create short videos for free. One of these is www.animoto.com. For authors and publishers who choose to make their own book video, it is important to use royalty free photos and music. Royalty free stock photo images can be found on such sites as www.freedigitalphotos.net and http://us.fotolia.com. Royalty free music can be found at www.openmusicarchive.org and www.partnersinrhyme.com. When creating a book video, remember to keep it short. Viewers have short attention spans. The best rule is to keep a book video under two minutes in length; 30 seconds is ideal.

Book videos need to be posted multiple places on the Internet to generate interest and be viewed by consumers. Your book video should be posted on multiple video sharing sites. Remember, posting is free publicity. Following are some good places to start.

Post It on Your Websites

Post the book video on the websites for the book's author and publisher, as well as the website for the book itself. Don't bury it in back pages, paste the video or a link to the video directly on the home page of your website.

Upload It to Your Social Networking Sites

Almost all social networking sites allow members to post videos on their page. Upload your book video to your page on each of your social networking sites. Your friends can view it and if they think it's great, they may share it with their friends. That's how things end up going viral on the Internet. There is no guarantee that your book video will go viral, but it doesn't even have a chance if you don't post it.

Place It on Book Video Sites

There are websites that are dedicated solely to showcasing book previews in video format on the web. These sites are growing as book videos become more popular. Placement of your book videos on these sites are free, again offering you free promotional opportunities for your book.

Following are some book video websites:

- www.christianbookvideos.com
- www.previewthebook.com
- www.bookriot.tv
- www.indytrailers.com
- www.bookreels.com
- http://booktrailercentral.com

Post It on General Video Sharing Sites

When video sharing sites (also known as video content communities) are mentioned, most people think of YouTube. YouTube is the most popular of the video sharing sites and it is growing by 100 hours of video every minute. However, there are a number of other viable video sharing sites that you can also put your book video on for people to discover and view.

Popular video sharing sites include:

- www.youtube.com
- www.vimeo.com
- www.godtube.com
- www.flickr.com
- www.dailymotion.com

In addition to video sharing sites, you can upload your book video to Amazon.com and other online bookstores that allow book videos.

Take a Virtual Book Tour

For many authors, a traditional book tour is too time consuming and expensive. Taking a virtual book tour is a great alternative. Virtual book tours, also known as blog tours, can expose your books to a large audience without costing you anything but your time.

A blog tour consists of an author "making an appearance" on a series of blogs over a few days or weeks. These appearances can take the form of a guest post on the blog by the author, an interview on the blog with the author (either written or podcast), a review of the book, an excerpt of a book, an interactive chat with the blog's audience, or any combination of these. Author appearances on a blog generally also include a picture of the cover of the book, a photo of the author, and a link to either the author's website or a website where the book can be purchased.

Guest Post: In a guest post, an author drafts a column for the blog. The column is usually related in some way to the subject matter of the book and relevant to the blog's audience.

Interview: The most common interview is a print interview between the blogger and the author. The blogger sends the author a series of questions via email to which the author responds. These questions and answers are then posted on the host blog for the blog audience to read.

Review of Book: Blog tours can include a review of your book on one or more blog sites. Some blog sites prefer to review books rather than host an interview or guest blog. Including blogs that only provide a review of your book in a blog tour increases the number of blogs you can make an appearance on for a virtual book tour.

Excerpt of Book: Some blogs choose to post a chapter excerpt from an author's book to entice the blog audience to consider purchasing the book. Excerpts are the least common type of post for author appearances on a blog.

Interactive Chat: Many blogs will host an interactive chat in their discussion room with the author in conjunction with a guest interview. An interactive chat allows the blog audience to post questions to an author and receive a virtual response by the author on the blog.

What's in it for the blog? Author appearances provide bloggers with material for their blog. That's material that they do not have to spend time generating, allowing them to increase their blog activity which generally leads to increased blog traffic. Hosting author appearances can also provide bloggers with a small amount of revenue since most use some type of affiliate link for their readers to purchase the book.

Arranging a Blog Tour

A blog book tour requires initiative on the part of an author or publicist. Generally bloggers will not come knocking on your door asking you for an appearance on their blog. Authors and publicists must reach out to bloggers and request them to host an online appearance.

The best way to initiate a blog tour is to begin with a blog search. Search the Internet for blogs that speak to the audience your book targets. For example, if you have a book of marriage advice for couples, search for blogs that write on this topic.

A blog search engine is your best bet for finding blogs. Numerous Blog search engines are available on the web. Some of these engines are:

- http://blogsearch.google.com
- www.blogsearchengine.com
- http://technorati.com
- www.globeofblogs.com

Simply type in your subject matter and the search engine will spew out a list of blogs that have recent posts on this subject.

To determine which blog sites may be a good match for your book, visit the blog sites acquired from your blog search. Check to make sure that the blogger posts blogs regularly and that the readers post comments frequently. If a blog has both a good blog activity level and reader involvement, then you will also want to check the traffic volume of the blog site. Finding out how many visitors a blog site has will keep you from wasting your time on blogs that only have a few visitors a week. One good place to check a blog's website traffic is www.alexa.com.

Once you have a list of potential blog sites, contact the bloggers via email. In your email, introduce yourself and your book, and request an author appearance. When requesting an author appearance, offer to do an interview, to provide an excerpt of your book, to write a guest blog column, or ask the blogger to review your book. Always offer the blogger a free copy of your book if they are interested in having you appear on their blog. It is also helpful to have posted on your author's website a cover photo of your book, a description of your book, an excerpt from your book, an author photo, and an author biography. Then in your email to a blogger, you can include a link to this information so that the blogger can learn more about you and your book.

Often offering a free book or two for the blogger to give away to their readers is a good hook. Many bloggers like to offer a free copy of the books they are featuring.

Blog Tour Services

If doing the research to arrange a blog tour sounds too time consuming for your current schedule, there are some publicity companies that specialize in scheduling blog tours for authors. Of course, these services always come with a price tag. A few companies that provide these services are listed below.

- **Christian Fiction Blog Alliance (CFBA)**
  CFBA runs three-day blog tours for Christian fiction books. All blog tours are listed in CFBA's *Christian Fiction Online Magazine*, http://christianfictiononlinemagazine.com, which is available free on the Internet as a resource for churches, book clubs, libraries, and bookstores.
  http://christianfictionblogalliance.com

- **FIRST (Fiction In Rather Short Takes) Wild Card Tours**
  This service helps authors and publishers schedule a blog tour for fiction books. FIRST features the first chapter of the book being toured so blog readers get a taste of the product.
  http://firstwildcardtours.blogspot.com

- **Pump Up Your Book**
  This public relations company specializes in online book promotion. They have a number of different blog tours and promotional packages to choose from.
  www.pumpupyourbook.com

- **Christian Science Fiction & Fantasy Blog Tour**
  This tour service specializes in Christian speculative fiction.
  http://csffblogtour.com

Optimize Amazon's Author Central

Amazon is the largest seller of books on the Internet. Over a quarter of all books purchased are bought on Amazon.com, accounting for 30% of all book dollars spent. Amazon provides free, worldwide exposure to those readers most likely to buy your books. Authors and publishers can use the tools Amazon provides to gain more exposure for books.

The main tool for authors on Amazon is called Amazon Author Central. To use this tool, your books must be listed on Amazon's website. Author Central allows authors to have a personal author page on Amazon, giving eligible authors another avenue to be found on both the Internet and Amazon, increasing your potential for more book sales.

Authors can register for free at https://authorcentral.amazon.com. Amazon screens anyone registering to ensure each person is a legitimate author on their website. This is done through validating each author's work with their publisher, generally via an email request.

Authors can create content on an Author Page via Author Central to increase their visibility. Amazon Customers find author pages in one of two ways: a book's product page provides a direct link to the author page (by clicking on the author's name), and the author page comes up as a result when someone searches for an author's name on Amazon.

Authors can optimize an Author Page on Amazon by making sure to include the following elements on their page.

Photo: Authors can upload a current photograph of themselves for their author page on Amazon. Making sure a good author photo is included in your author page increases your recognition factor for readers. Readers like to know what an author looks like. Many authors feel that having their picture on a book encourages a connection with readers. People are visual. Seeing a photo with a name helps people remember the person, and, as an author, you want to be remembered.

Biography: Amazon allows authors to write a biography about themselves and place this on their author page. Biographies tell readers why you are qualified to write on a certain topic. For fiction authors, biographies create a connection for the reader to the author of the book, helping to turn a reader into a fan. If you have an author website or a website dedicated to a book, be sure to include the URLs for your websites in your biography.

Bibliography: A bibliography simply lists all the books an author has penned. Listing all your titles on your Author Page helps introduce readers to other books you have written; potentially leading to additional sales. Amazon's Author Page only allows authors to list those books that are available on Amazon. The process is easy. Amazon has you search for your books and then you simply click on the book results you want listed on your author page.

Import Your Blog: Amazon allows you to import your blog posts to your Author Page. All you have to do is plug in the RSS feed from your blog under the Author Central "Blog" tab where it says, "Add an RSS Feed." Then, readers who may not know about your blog can find it on your Amazon

Author Page. Each blog post that appears has a link to take the reader directly to your actual blog page to read each entry.

List Your Events: Authors can add events they are hosting or appearing at to their Author Page on Amazon. Simply click on the "Events" tab on your Amazon Author Central home page and manually input the upcoming events that you want to advertise.

Videos: Do you have a book trailer? What about a video of you promoting your book? Amazon allows authors to upload videos to their Author Pages. If you have videos that promote your books, you can upload them to your Amazon Author Page. Simply click on the "Videos" button under your Author Central home page and follow the directions. Remember, videos are a great way to draw readers' interest to your books.

Customer Discussions: There is a place on each author's page for customer discussions. This section allows customers to ask questions, share opinions, and get insights. Authors can start a discussion on their home page, or use this discussion section to as a communication tool to let readers know information related to their books.

Book Reviews: Authors who want to generate more exposure for their books can write reviews of other books in their book's genre and post these reviews on Amazon.com. Your reviews should include a signature line with your name and "author of ..." listing your book. People who are interested in books in your genre will then be directed to your book when they read your Amazon review of another book.

BlogTalkRadio

Smartphones and tablets have heralded a new age of online radio listeners. BlogTalkRadio (www.blogtalkradio.com) recognized this trend back in 2006, and set up an interactive online platform for two-way conversations that could be accessed by telephone and broadcast over the Internet. Today, BlogTalkRadio is the largest enabler of user-generated audio content on the Internet. The platform has 1,800 shows created every day with 40,000,000 people listening each month.

Best of all, BlogTalkRadio is free to use or listen to. Here is how it works. A BlogTalkRadio show host logs on to their show-designated page on the BlogTalkRadio website. The host sets the time he wants his show to air. Then using a telephone (land or cell) the host calls a special number. Guests and listeners can also call the number. The number is generally a New York number; so long distance charges are the responsibility of the caller (host, guest, and audience call-ins). The host can put as many as five people on the air at one. This set-up is very conducive to interviewing a guest or two and accepting on-air questions from listeners. While only five people can be on the air at one time, an unlimited number of people can listen to the show, which is streamed from the BlogTalkRadio website. The show is then archived as a podcast which can be streamed online or downloaded to a computer or listening device. In addition, BlogTalkRadio provides promotional badges and flash player code for placements of shows on blogs and social networking sites.

Consider the following ways you can use BlogTalkRadio to increase the exposure for your books.

Start Your Own BlogTalkRadio Show

Hosting a show on BlogTalkRadio to promote the books you publish is a great way to increase exposure for your books. Interviews with other authors and experts related to your books' topics can help you collect a following of loyal fans who will tell others about your show and your books.

BlogTalkRadio is the largest enabler of user-generated audio content.

While it is free to host a show on BlogTalkRadio, it does take time. The site features tutorials to teach users how to host a show. One of the nice features of BlogTalkRadio is that shows do not have to be on a regular basis. You can choose to host one show a month or four a year. If, however, you are looking to build an audience and a following through a radio show, airing new shows on a regular basis is a requisite.

Become a Guest on BlogTalkRadio Shows

In addition to hosting your own show, you can get exposure for your books to new audiences through guest appearances on existing BlogTalkRadio shows. There are a number of hosts on BlogTalkRadio who are in need of new guests on a regular basis. BlogTalkRadio allows users to search for shows based on subject matter. Use your book's subject to find hosts who discuss that issue and then email the host of each show to see if they would be interested in hosting you for an interview.

Advertise on BlogTalkRadio Shows

BlogTalkRadio has a revenue sharing program with their show hosts. Revenue sharing encourages hosts to allow ads on their shows. The host then receives a portion of the revenue from the ads. Publishers and authors can place advertisements on BlogTalkRadio. Ads can be placed by show or by category depending on the type of campaign an advertiser wants to run.

This helps you create a targeted ad campaign, allowing you to reach just the audience your book is intended for. BlogTalkRadio provides information on their advertising programs on their website.

QR Codes

QR codes, which stands for Quick Response codes, allow you to integrate your print marketing with the Internet. These postage-stamp size matrixes continue to gain momentum as smartphone owners grow across the globe. The latest statistics show that an average of one out of every five people has scanned a QR code.

> No longer do consumers need to remember URLs.

QR Codes consists of black squares arranged in a pattern on a white background. A QR code gives anyone with a smart phone quick access to additional information. Via a QR code app, consumers can use the camera on their cell phone or tablet to scan the code and connect directly to the webpage the code is designed to transport the user to.

QR codes have become quite popular. No longer do consumers need to remember URL addresses or names of books, companies, or items. All they need is a smart phone to read a QR code and the phone does all the work. Since QR codes link the user to a website, you can use them in a variety of ways to sell your products. In addition to posting a long website address that your audience is likely to forget by the time they get to their computer, place a QR code on your printed materials. Whether it's an advertisement, direct mail, business card, flyer, or exterior street signage, your potential consumer can immediately gain access to what you're promoting, and you can nudge them to act now instead of possibly later.

The marketing possibilities with QR codes are endless. You can use a QR code on a mailer or postcard to take the consumer to a webpage featuring a coupon or coupon code for your advertised special. Place it on your business cards so people don't have to type in or remember your website or use it to connect people to your LinkedIn or Facebook profile. You can also place a code on the back cover copy of your next book. The code can take the reader to the book's website, trailer, or the author's blog.

QR codes are free to generate, so you can use them on all your printed promotional materials. Just head on over to ZumoTools (www.zumoqr.com) or BeQRious (http://beqrious.com/generator), and create one. These sites allow you to link your QR Code to a website, email address, phone number, a text message, or to a YouTube video. In addition, for a fee, BeQRious allows you to track how many people scan your QR code.

Creative Marketing

The Internet provides authors and publishers many opportunities for creative marketing and books. Two ideas are listed here, although there are many more.

Craigslist

Craigslist (www.craigslist.com) offers publishers and authors free classified ad postings to market and sell more of your books. Created in 1995, Craigslist is the largest classified advertisement site on the Internet, and one of the top 100 websites worldwide. The site hosts local classified ads in 70 countries around the world. Publishers and authors can post advertisements for their books under the "books" category on Craigslist. Strategic cities can be targeted or you can run a circulating ad campaign encompassing a number of cities. With Craigslist, the seller can choose to remain anonymous, so no personal information is given out. A link can be placed in the ad where the buyer can purchase the books directly from your website, Amazon, or another online bookseller, so there is no need for you to be contacted directly. Through posting advertisements for you books on Craigslist, you can potentially reach an audience you might not otherwise touch with your traditional marketing campaign.

Expert Sites

Any author that has written a book on a subject is automatically considered to be an expert on that subject. After all, you should know quite a bit about a particular subject before you pen a book on it. Authors can take advantage of their expertise to promote their books. One way is to offer advice online. Expert sites give authors the opportunity to do this and draw attention to their book on the subject. There are a number of newer social-based question and answer sites where all members can ask and answer questions. These sites include www.Quora.com, www.Answers.com, and www.JustAnswer.com. By joining one or more of these sites, authors can answer questions in their areas of expertise and broaden their online connections, exposing new potential customers to their books.

Summary

An Internet presence has become an essential ingredient in success for book producers. The Internet is vast and the opportunities it holds for promotion are endless. Creative use of the Internet can lead to great promotional ideas that, in today's day and age, spread rapidly among Internet users. Whole books are dedicated to this subject. While this chapter has barely scratched the surface of harnessing the Internet to promote your books, hopefully it has at least served to get you started on the path to promoting your Christian books on the Internet.

14

Leverage Social Networking

*Each of you should look not only to your own interest,
but also to the interest of others.*
—Philippians 2:4

> Marketing Fundamental:
> **The best marketing is relational.**

It is a tough bookselling market. More books are being published today than ever before. The task of every author and publisher is to get their books noticed in a noisy world. To this end, you must be creative and use every means available to reach your target audience. One way to reach your audience is by hanging out where your audience hangs out and one of the main places people are hanging out today is on social networking sites (also called social media).

Social media is the number one activity on the Internet. Nine out of ten Internet users are on a social networking site, and one out of every five minutes spent online is on a social networking site. It is changing our world.

Even the way people discover new books is shifting as a result of social networking. Just a few years ago, one-third of new books were discovered in physical bookstores. Now that number has shrunk to one-fifth, while digital discovery of books is increasing. Today, at least one in six new books is discovered online in some form.

At least one in six new books is discovered online.

Publishers and authors can use social networking to connect with potential readers, increase publicity, and extend the scope of exposure for their books. The social networking "Rule of 30" says that 30 posts in 30 days read by 30 people exposes you, your ideas, and your book to up to 900 people. This is what social networking is about: growing your connections.

Basically, any site that is interactive—that allows users to comment and interact with the material—is defined as a social media site. This chapter will look at the most popular social networking sites, but will start with the rules of engagement in social networking.

Rules of Engagement

The goal of social networking is to create an increased presence on the web so that you can extend the visibility of your book, and thus your marketing reach. The best part about using it to promote your books is that it is free.

However, social media is not traditional advertising. You cannot shout about your books on social networking sites. Many authors use social media to try to promote their books without understanding the fundamental difference between traditional advertising and marketing on social media.

With traditional advertising, businesses show off their products. Think about advertisements that you have seen on television, heard on the radio, or read in magazines and newspapers or on billboards. Consider the direct mail postcards and flyers you receive in your snail mailbox. All of these advertisements shout about the product. They all say, "Look at this," and "Buy this product."

Social media marketing does not use traditional marketing strategies. Social media is conversation-based. Think of social media as a large social gathering, much like a party. At a party, savvy individuals do not go up to strangers and say, "Hi, I'm an author and you should buy my book." Rather, individuals engage in small talk and find common ground to converse about. If an opportunity presents itself, an individual will often divulge what they do for a living. If the other party in the conversation is interested in learning more, they will ask for more information.

Sarah Bolme

That's the way social media works. It's a conversation. If you are going to use social media to market your products, be conversational. Don't shout about your books. Rather, engage with others. Listen and respond. Add value to others' lives by sharing information that is interesting and useful.

Once people have made a connection with you, then they will be interested in what you do. Only then will they be open to hearing about and looking at the books you write or publish. Social media is not just about showing off your products. It is about connecting with individuals. Connections build trust. Trust builds confidence. Confidence brings readers.

So be human on social media. Engage in conversation, share interesting information, and book sales will follow.

Blogs

Blogs are personal journals of thoughts, ideas, and advice posted on the web. These personal journals are generally updated daily or weekly with the blog author's opinions and musings. Blogs were one of the first forms of social networking on the Internet because blogs allow for readers to make comments directly on the blog for all the other readers of that blog to read and respond to.

Blogs are popular and influential. There are over 181 million blogs on the Internet. Studies show that 77% of Internet users read blogs. Each month, 337 million people read 2.5 billion blog pages just on one blog platform—WordPress.com. Blogs hold a lot of influence over purchasing decisions of consumers. Studies show that blogs rank third (behind retail sites and brand sites) in impacting consumers' decision to purchase a product. Consumers report that blogs rank higher than Twitter for shaping their opinions and higher than Facebook for motivating purchasing decisions. On top of that, 87% of blog readers are book buyers!

Authors can use a blog to build an audience for their books. Creating a blog is free. You can place a blog on your existing website, or you can use a free blogging platform such as www.blogspot.com or www.wordpress.com to host your blog. If your existing website already generates a substantial amount of traffic, then adding a blog on your website can serve to keep your customers coming back as well as generate additional traffic. If your website could use a boost in traffic, then creating a blog can potentially bring new traffic to your existing website and widen the audience for your books.

The two greatest challenges with a blog are developing regular posts for your blog and generating a following of people who read your blog regularly.

Generating Material for a Blog

Blogs require new material at regular intervals to keep a steady following of readers. The more frequent the posts, the more readers a blog will generally acquire. Studies show that blogs that post every day have the largest number of followers. While most authors don't have the time to post to their blog every day, generating new content at least weekly is best. However, coming up with new and interesting material for a blog is always a challenge.

If you are an author, your blog should tie into the theme of your books. While you can blog about your writing process and upcoming writing projects, placing ongoing new information, news, and advice related to the subject of your books will keep your fans engaged.

Having other experts in your subject be guests on your blog is a good way to add to your content. Other authors or individuals with some expertise on your subject are usually willing to provide guest posts as these give the author expanded exposure. One place to find experts willing to provide you with guest posts is through the Blogger Linkup service (www.bloggerlinkup.com). This free service allows bloggers to place and receive requests for guest posts.

Reviewing books with a subject matter similar to yours on your blog is another way to generate material for your blog. Blogging is not just about promoting your own books. It is about giving people information and adding value to their lives. The more value you provide others, the more they will respect what you have to offer.

Building an Audience

The Internet is a busy place. Multiple websites are vying for people's attention. Creating a blog that stands out and gets attention will take work. Finding an audience for your blog is much like finding an audience for your book. It will take marketing. Experts report that it takes nine months to develop a good readership base for a blog.

Authors can list their blog on their books to alert readers where to go for more great information from the author. Announcing a blog to your email list and on all your other social networking sites is also useful in acquiring readers.

One way of finding new readership for your blog is to be a guest author on others' blogs. Many bloggers use guests to round out their blog offerings. You can create posts that can be used on other blogs that reach your target audience. Those blog readers that like your post will also begin to follow and read your blog. Blogger Linkup (www.bloggerlinkup.com) is a great place to find bloggers seeking articles.

Another way to find new readers for your blog is to join the conversation elsewhere. Find blogs that are related to your subject matter and make interesting and engaging comments on these posts. Remember, the etiquette for joining a digital conversation is no different than for joining a live conversation. Become a part of the existing conversation by commenting on what is already being discussed rather than just jumping in and pitching your book. Once you've become a part of the conversation, opportunities for sharing about your own blog or book will arise naturally.

Yet another way to generate new traffic for your blog is to take part in a blog carnival. A blog carnival is where a blogger collects blog posts on a given topic and puts all these posts together in one blog post called a "carnival." There are blog carnivals for every subject available. To be part of a blog carnival, you simply have to submit one of your blog posts to a carnival on your subject. To find a blog carnival to participate in, visit www.blogcarnival.com.

> Blogging is not just about promoting your own books. It's about adding value to people's lives.

Experts report that it takes about nine months of regular posting for a blog to develop a strong, loyal readership base. Just as with marketing, creating and maintaining a blog to enlarge your marketing reach will take time and dedication on your part.

Social Network Community Sites

The most popular social networking sites on the Internet are Facebook, Google+, Twitter, Pinterest, and LinkedIn. Every author should be using at least one of these free services to engage their readers and enlarge their marketing reach.

Facebook

Facebook is the top social networking site on the Internet and the second most visited website (right behind Google). With over one billion users, Facebook should be an integral part of any marketing plan for a book. Authors and publishers can use this tool to reach potential customers and stay in contact with fans. It's the easiest place to reach the most people in one swoop.

Facebook is a wonderful free tool for keeping your name and products in front of Christian book readers on a regular basis. Every author and publisher should have a Facebook business page (this is different from a personal profile on Facebook). To create a business page on Facebook, simply go to www.facebook.com and click on the "Create Page" link and follow the instructions.

Once you have a Facebook page, your next step is to collect fans for your page. Send out an email notice to your current subscription list notifying your customers that they can "Like" your Facebook page. Your website and blog should also include a link to your Facebook page so that visitors to your website can also "Like" you on Facebook.

After you have collected a few fans, use your Facebook page to engage your fans through interesting posts. Create connections and add value to your customers and potential customers' lives. Engagement is the name of the game on Facebook. Every post that you place on your Business page does not show up in all your fans' newsfeeds. Facebook only sends each post to a percentage of your fans. However, the more engagement (likes and comments) you receive on your posts, the more of your fans see your posts on their personal newsfeeds.

Facebook has a feature called "Boost Post" or "Promote Your Post" that allows you to pay a fee to enlarge the number of people who see a given post. Using the Promote Your Post feature can be effective advertising on Facebook and allow you to collect more fans and enlarge the scope of your marketing reach.

Experts recommend that you start by creating one post a day for your Business page. Make sure your posts engage your fans, not just push your books. Once you have fans engaging with your posts, then you can increase your daily posts if you want. Don't post too often (more than three times per day) or you may cluttering people's newsfeeds and end up losing fans as a result. Remember, your goal is to engage your fans. Here are a few suggestions:

- Engage your fans with polls and questions.
- Comment on news stories that relate to your books' topics.
- Announce new books.
- Report on upcoming events.
- Hold contests for book giveaways.
- Offer Facebook-only special discounts.
- Highlight your author events.
- Add value by giving your fans resources related to your books' unique topics.
- Post serious and silly pictures and videos related to your books.

Keep in mind that social media is not a sales channel. Rather, it is a light marketing tool. Social networking helps you keep your books in front of potential customers, increasing the likelihood that they not only purchase and read your book, but also share it with others.

Pinterest

Pinterest is somewhat different from other social networking sites. Basically, Pinterest is a giant virtual bulletin board. Users collect, post, and share their favorite ideas, pictures, and products by "pinning" images with short descriptions on their Pinterest page. People use Pinterest to plan their weddings, decorate their homes, share books they are reading, and organize their favorite recipes.

Like other social media sites, users collect followers and share "pins" on their virtual bulletin board (called Boards). Anyone can browse Boards on Pinterest and discover new things, as well as get inspiration from other people who share their interests. Many companies are using Pinterest for better customer engagement because this new site allows them to engage customers in a visually interesting way.

To create a profile on Pinterest, simply go to www.pinterest.com and sign up. Then, similar to Facebook, you can start collecting followers by letting your existing circle of influence know that they can follow you on Pinterest.

Be sure to install the "Pin It" button to your web browser. This lets you grab an image from any website around the Internet and quickly add it to one of your Boards on Pinterest. You can find the "Pin It" button at https://about.pinterest.com/goodies.

The fundamentals for using Pinterest to promote your books are similar to any other social media website. A few to keep in mind are:

- Add a "Follow me on Pinterest" button to your website (similar to the buttons you have for Facebook and Twitter).
- Connect your Pinterest account to your Facebook and Twitter accounts to gain more followers and for maximum exposure.
- Pin content steadily rather than in huge bursts. This keeps your engagement continual.
- Use interesting and engaging names for your boards.
- Descriptive content for an image pinned is capped at 500 characters. The intent is to send interested parties to an image's original website for more information.
- Comment on and "Like" other people's pins just like on other social media sites.
- Keep some variety in your pins. Don't just pin about your products, pin also about topics related to your books.
- Pin your own blog posts to gain wider exposure.

Pinterest is an effective tool. Pinterest's users buy things. Pinterest users spend more money, more often, on more items than any of the other top five social media sites. Almost half (47%) of online consumers in the United States have made a purchase based on recommendations from Pinterest. This social networking site offers publishers and authors another free Internet marketing tool to gain more traction for their books.

Twitter

Twitter boasts 215 million active monthly users. While Twitter is generally referred to as a social networking site and is always included in the suggested basic elements of a good social media strategy for businesses, a study by a group of researchers in Korea concluded that Twitter is not really a social network. After analyzing over 41 million user profiles and 106 million tweets, the researchers concluded that only 22% of the connections on Twitter are reciprocal. Rather, the majority (78%) of connections between users on Twitter are one-way relationships. The conclusion these researchers came to is that Twitter is more of a broadcast medium than a social network. It turns out that many people use Twitter as a news medium to follow breaking news.

Knowing that Twitter acts more like a news medium than a social network does not change the fact that it should be part of your online marketing strategy. It still remains a powerful tool for book promotion.

Twitter is very popular. As the tenth most visited website on the Internet it is a useful tool for enlarging your reach. Twitter can help to keep your books in front of people and generate traffic to your website or blog.

To get started using Twitter just go to www.twitter.com and sign up. Then, create a customized page and start following other Twitter users. In addition to letting your existing social network followers know that you are now on Twitter, you can collect followers by registering your Twitter account in directories of Twitter users:

- www.twibs.com
- www.twibes.com
- www.tweetfind.com
- www.wefollow.com

People use these directories to find other Twitter users with similar interests to follow. When registering your business on directories, be sure to use key words that best fit with the people in your target audience. For example, you might want to use "Christian" as one of your category tabs.

Think of Twitter as a communication tool. Remember, it's a news feed, so use Twitter to give information about your books as well as about the topics in your books. You can announce upcoming events, new blog posts, specials on your books, breaking news on your books' topics, and ideas to improve people's Christian lives. Remember, Twitter messages (tweets) are short and to the point. You only have 140 characters to communicate.

With short messages, Twitter has developed its own command language. To address a specific person, the @ sign is placed in front of the person's Twitter name. A # sign (called a hashtag) is placed in front of a subject word. This allows people to look for all the tweets about a certain subject (such as #Christian or #Obama).

Twitter is a streaming conversation. People using Twitter do not go back for hours to read all the tweets that come across their timeline. They tend to skim the messages and read those that catch their interest, or else they follow their interests through hashtags. You will have the most potential for success in connecting with people by tweeting a few times a day. With too few tweets, your efforts may be ineffective. On the flip side, too many tweets (more than 12 per day), may turn your followers off.

> Twitter is more of a broadcast medium than a social network.

Remember, people generally expect to gain information or be entertained from their social networks. So, be sure that you are adding value (giving good information) to the people you are trying to reach with your tweets.

Google+

Google+ is the backbone of Google. While not as large as Facebook, it is a social media site where your active participation is practically mandatory if you want to beat your competitors in Google's search results. Authors, in particular, need to promote their name and books via this social site.

Google is beginning to pay less attention to keywords in its search results. In essence, the role of SEO is changing as search engines change. In other words, the days of gaming search engines with keywords may soon be over. Rather, Google's search engine algorithms are looking more at engagement and quality content in determining placement in a search result.

Google is king of the Internet. It has the corner on web searches, with 81% of searches using their service. Google ties all their brand pages into their search engine. Basically, Google has said that information tied to verified online profiles on Google+ will be ranked higher than content without such verification. In other words, ignore Google+ and Google will ignore you.

Google wants full engagement. Therefore, creating a profile on Google+ and posting is only half the equation. The other half is adding Google+ to your website or blog. You will get even better traction in Google's search engine if you add your Google+ profile badge to your websites.

One of the helpful tools on Google+ is the ability to chat with others. Twitter allows authors to chat with readers—all in text. Authors can chat with followers on Facebook—all in text. Google+ has a video chat feature called Hangouts, which allows authors to chat with individuals in their Google+ circles via video.

Google Hangouts has two settings users can access: Hangouts Party and Hangouts on Air. All Hangouts can be watched live, but they can also be archived on YouTube, the second largest search engine—behind only Google itself—making your content that much easier for users to find. Google Hangouts Party video chat is limited to 10 people participating. However, if you want to do a Google Hangouts for people to watch an author reading the first chapter of an upcoming book, then you would use Hangouts on Air rather than Hangouts Party. With a Google Hangouts on Air, your video broadcast is available to anyone that want to watch—essentially, a YouTube recording of your Hangouts is made as it is happening, allowing anyone to watch.

Some authors are switching to Google Hangouts on Air for their webinars. Rather than using www.GoToWebinar.com or www.Webex.com, they are choosing Google Hangouts on Air because it has more features. With Google Hangouts on Air, presenters have the ability to share slides as in a traditional webinar format, but it also allows the presenter's face to be shown. In addition, Google has been adding a number of features to Hangouts on Air including a question and answer app and other audience tools.

If you are already using Facebook, Twitter, LinkedIn, or Pinterest, learning to use Google+ will not be difficult. It operates much like these other social networking sites. You can tag people on Google+ using the @ sign, just like Twitter, and hashtags (#subject) are also used. Google+ has circles, so you can create a "friends" circle, a "family" circle, a "following" circle, etc. The possibilities for circles are limitless. As with the other social networking sites, all the same rules apply: post regularly, mind your manners, add value, and be social.

Book Social Networking

Booklovers love great books and they love to share those books with friends. When the boon of social networking began on the Internet, specialty sites arose to reach different populations. One type of these social networking specialty sites were book social networks that arose for booklovers to meet and talk about the books they are reading and want to read.

While book networking sites are not sites for authors to sell their books, as an author you can take advantage of the social connections these sites provide to spread the word about the books you have published.

The main book social networking sites are:

- **Goodreads**
  www.goodreads.com

- **Shelfari**
  www.shelfari.com

- **LibraryThing**
  www.librarything.com

- **JacketFlap**
  www.jacketflap.com

- **Revish**
  www.revish.com

Each of these book social networking sites offers ways for authors to promote their books. Many have similar programs.

Goodreads

Goodreads, which is now owned by Amazon.com, is the largest of all the book social networking sites with 10 million users. It is twice as large as LibraryThing and Shelfari combined. Every author should join this network and take advantage of the opportunities available for promoting your books. Goodreads offers an Author Program designed to help authors reach their target audience—passionate readers. The Goodreads Author Program can help you get the word out about your books.

Author Profile Pages: An Author Profile page on Goodreads is much like a profile page on any other social networking site. This profile allows you to list the books you have authored, post updates, import a blog, and connect with readers. With your author profile page, you can post excerpts from your books to entice the people you connect with to check out your books.

List a Book Giveaway to Generate Pre-Launch Buzz: Goodreads allows authors to give away a few print copies of an upcoming book. They list the book on their Giveaways page and Goodreads members enter to receive a free copy of the book. At the end of the giveaway period (specified by the author or publisher) Goodreads selects a winner at random. The average Goodreads book giveaway garners 750 entries. Many of those readers who do not receive the book will go on to read it and post a review on Goodreads at some point in time after the book is released.

Advertise Your Book: Goodreads offers advertising on their site on a cost-per-click basis. You can set the amount of money you are willing to pay per month (much like GoogleAds or Facebook ads) and design an ad for your book. These ads run on the home page, search page, and a few other places where Goodreads members browse for books. In addition, you can target your ads to the people you want to see it.

While Goodreads is not targeted exclusively to Christian readers, many readers on the site are Christians and read and review Christian books. If you are looking to reach a dedicated group of readers, Goodreads is a good bet.

Join Online Communities

Joining online communities is another good way to promote yourself and your books. Online communities exist for every target audience you can think of. These communities host chat rooms, discussion forums, discussion groups, articles, and helpful links; they publish e-newsletters and feature advertisements. Joining those communities that represent your target audience is a great marketing strategy.

Online communities are free to join and present many opportunities for publishers and authors to promote books. Authors and publishers can join online communities that match their books' subjects and find opportunities to promote their books through article submissions and discussion boards. You can also take advantage of the advertising opportunities on these community sites.

There are too many online communities to list here. Below is a sample of online communities geared toward one population: Christian moms.

- www.christianmom.com
- www.momsoffaith.com
- www.christian-mommies.com
- www.circleofmoms.com

A Word of Caution

The effectiveness of your social networking will largely depend on what you do. Social networking can be time consuming. It is easy to get sucked in and spend inordinate amounts of time being social on the Internet. A time management plan or strategy for how much time you will spend social networking and where that time will be spent will go a long way towards helping you not to waste your valuable time. Remember, social networking is only one component of an overall effective marketing plan and thus should be treated as any other marketing strategy: with thoughtfulness and prudence.

Social media is changing daily. New sites and trends appear and disappear regularly. Whole books are devoted to teaching people how to use social media to promote businesses. This chapter is simply a brief introduction to the use of social media to promote books.

Summary

Even though social media is one of the most powerful ways for authors to engage with people and promote books, it is not the only way. Since social media is free to use, some authors are tempted to make it their only marketing avenue. Don't fall into this trap. Rather, incorporate social media into your overall strategy, making its percentage of your marketing strategy proportional to its effectiveness.

Handle Overstocks and Remainders

*There is a time for everything, and
a season for every activity under heaven.*
—Ecclesiastes 3:1

> Marketing Fundamental:
> **Good businesses have a contingency plan.**

Sometimes, despite your best efforts, a title does not sell as well as you anticipated. What is a publisher to do with too much inventory? Excess inventory can come in the form of remainders (books left over when you have discontinued a title) or overstocks (extra books taking up needed storage space).

While most publishers today are using print-on-demand technology allowing them better manage their inventory, those that use offset printing may face the dilemma of winding up with extra inventory. If you end up with excess inventory on your hands that you wish to find a home for, there are three options at your disposal.

One option is to sell these books to a bargain book company. Another option is to gift your overstock or remainder books to a nonprofit organization. The third option is to throw the books into the recycle bin. Most authors and publishers love books and are loath to choose this third option. That is why this chapter is devoted to helping you to navigate selling your books to a bargain book company at a heavily discounted price or donating them to a charity.

Bargain Book Companies

Bargain book companies are a thriving industry. One of the strategies CBA has been promoting to member retail stores to help them draw in customers is to have a bargain book center in the store. Bargain book companies purchase remainders, overstocks, and damaged skids and then sell these books to retailers to sell at highly discounted prices: generally between 80 to 90 percent off the listed retail price. Of course, this means these companies buy your overstock, remainders, and damaged skids for pennies per book.

Here is how it usually works. You submit a copy of the title that you want to liquidate to a bargain book company with information on how many you have available for them to purchase. The company then gives you an offer on the books. If you accept the offer, the bargain book company pays you cash on delivery of your books (they also pay for the shipping). When selling books to a remainder company, it is wise to mark the books with a small black mark, usually near the price. This way, a store cannot return the book to you or your wholesale company as a "return" for credit against their account.

Below are bargain book companies that sell to the Christian retail marketplace. When contacting a company, simply ask to speak to a buyer. If you need to liquidate overstock or damaged skids for books that you are still actively selling in the Christian retail market, you may want to choose a bargain book company that sells to the secular marketplace, as most retail stores will not stock your title at normal price and also have it in the bargain book center. With some bargain book companies, you can specify which particular stores you do not want your book sold to so that there is no crossover from your sales and the bargain book company's greatly reduced prices to the Christian retail marketplace.

- **Bargain Books Wholesale**
  Bargain Books Wholesale sells to both the secular and the Christian retail marketplace.
  Bargain Books Wholesale
  3030 29th St. SE
  Grand Rapids, MI 49512
  717-227-9576
  www.bargainbookswholesale.com

- **Book Depot**
  This is a book wholesaler in Canada that sells mostly to the Canadian market. They also sell books direct to the public at bargain prices on their website.
  Book Depot
  67 Front Street North
  Thorold, Ontario, L2V 1X3
  Canada
  905-680-7230
  www.bookdepot.com

- **Inspirational Closeout Solutions**
  This company specializes in discount Christian books. They sell to the general trade, CBA independent and chain stores, mass market stores, and international accounts. This company also allows publishers to direct products to the channel of your choice, therefore protecting bargain titles from competing with front-line sales channels.
  Inspirational Closeout Solutions
  PO Box 3038
  Knoxville, TN 37927
  262-898-4440
  www.icsrep.com

- **Wholesale Christian Books**
  This large company has a showroom in New York City. They specialize in selling bargain and discount books to Christian stores, bargain outlets, dollar stores, and other discount chains. Wholesale Christian Books sells the books to these retailers for 8% off of retail price so that the retailers can sell the books at 50% off of retail price and retain a good profit.

Wholesale Christian Books
2745 Chicory Rd.
Racine, WI 53403
770-401-2103
www.wholesalechristianbooks.com

The Christian market no longer hosts a bargain book show. Rather, bargain book sellers generally exhibit at the International Christian Retail Show (ICRS) to attract new retail customers.

The general market has two bargain book shows: CIROBE (www.cirobe.com) and GABBS, formerly the Spring Book Show (www.gabbs.net). Retailers from around the world come to these shows to purchase bargain books for their stores. Publishers and remainder companies display at these shows to sell bargain books directly to bookstores for resale. Most small publishers and independently published authors would not find it cost effective to display at one of these shows as your inventory would be extremely limited. Thus, using a bargain book company to sell your books is the more efficient route.

Gifting Books to a Nonprofit Organization

There are a number of nonprofit organizations designed to receive and redistribute larger amounts of books to needy individuals for great causes. These organizations welcome boxes of overstock or remainder titles.

When you choose to gift books to a nonprofit organization, you do not get money for your books, but you can usually claim a tax deduction for books donated to a qualified 501(c)(3) nonprofit organization.

Here are some nonprofits that accept bulk book donations.

- **Christian Library International (CLI)**
  Christian Library International serves adult and youth prison inmates by providing Christian books to prisons, jails, and youth detention centers. The new and used materials are shipped directly to chaplains who distribute them by means of a lending library, a book cart, or by personally giving them to the inmates. If you want to donate multiple copies of one title, CLI asks that you send the book with a cover letter explaining your desire to donate more copies. Include your name, address, phone and email. Once CLI confirms that the book matches with their Statement of Faith and guidelines, they will contact you to proceed with the donation.

Christian Library International
3800 A Hillcrest Drive
Raleigh, NC 27610
919-212-8122
www.christianlibraryinternational.org

- **National Association for the Exchange of Industrial Resources (NAEIR)**
  This nonprofit association solicits donations of valuable, new merchandise from American companies and distributes the items to nonprofit organizations, churches, and schools to be used solely for the care of the ill, the needy, and minors.
  NAEIR
  560 McClure St.
  Galesburg, IL 61401
  800-562-0955
  www.naeir.org

- **OM Ships International**
  OM Ships International is the ship ministry that brings knowledge, help, and hope to the people of the world. Donated books are either used as literature for people in need or they are sold at bargain prices to Christian bookstores. The funds from these sales are used to support the ministry of OM Ships International.
  OM Ships International
  779 St. Andrews Rd.
  Florence, SC 29501
  843-667-9997
  www.books.omships.org

- **World Vision**
  World Vision is a Christian relief and development organization operating in 100 countries around the world including the United States. They are dedicated to helping children and their communities worldwide reach their full potential by tackling the causes of poverty. You can select which countries you want your books distributed to.
  World Vision
  Gifts-In-Kind Department
  888-511-6548
  www.worldvision.org/gik

Summary

Whether you choose to sell your remainder and overstock books to a bargain bookseller or gift them to a charity, your books can still have the impact of touching someone's life for eternal purposes. Even business disappointments can turn into spiritual successes through these means.

Part Three

Targeting Special Markets

eBooks

*He put a new song in my mouth, a hymn of praise to our God.
Many will see and fear and put their trust in the Lord.*
—Psalm 40:3

> **Marketing Fundamental:**
> **Staying abreast of technology
> keeps your marketing efforts viable.**

Over the past few years, book publishing has entered a new era. eBooks are now an integral part of producing and selling books. They have become a central figure in the book publishing and buying market.

Sales of ebooks continue to grow. Pricewaterhouse Coopers (PwC) has predicted that the U.S. ebook market will surpass the printed book market in 2017. Presently, just over a quarter of Americans currently buy ebooks and nearly half plan to do so in a year's time, according to a recent survey. The survey also found that about 22% of Americans don't plan to start reading ebooks any time in the next three years.

Today, savvy publishers understand the need for books to be produced in both print and digital format. One survey found that 86% of ebook publishers still produce a print version of every ebook title. As ebook sales continue to grow, making them a part of your sales mix is vital for success. Of course, the keys to selling digital books are the same as selling print books. Marketing is the most important tool in selling books because people can't buy books they don't know about.

Digital Publishing Trade Associations

eBook technology is rapidly progressing and changing. Publishers of ebooks must stay abreast of this technology to remain viable in the ebook market. While publishers and authors producing digital books can belong to any traditional publishers or authors association and receive great information, benefits, and networking opportunities, there are a couple of general-market trade associations specifically geared toward ebook authors and publishers that provide cutting-edge information and opportunities for this medium.

- **Digital Book World (DBW)**
  Once an annual conference addressing the radically changing digital publishing movement, DBW has evolved into a year-round platform offering educational and networking resources for consumer publishing professionals and their partners.
  www.digitalbookworld.com

- **Electronic Publishing Industry Coalition (EPIC)**
  EPIC exists to provide a strong voice for electronic publishing. Once an authors' organization, it has expanded to include professionals from all facets of the electronic publishing industry: authors, publishers, editors, artists, and others. Members work together to further the industry.
  www.epicorg.com

- **International Digital Publishing Forum (IDPF)**
  IDPF is a global trade and industry standards organization dedicated to the development and promotion of electronic publishing. IDPF welcomes book, magazine, journal, and newspaper publishers producing materials in the digital reading format to join the organization.
  www.idpf.org

eBook Distribution

As with print books, having your ebook available via Amazon.com is not enough. Selling an ebook from just your website or just Amazon.com will not make your book readily available to those who prefer a different reading platform such as the Apple iPad or the Nook tablet. Not everyone shops at Amazon. As with print books, having your ebooks listed for sale in multiple online bookstores will reap the most sales. Any momentum you build toward sales of your book can be cut short if your ebook is not easily accessible in multiple places online.

Amazon has about two-thirds of the U.S. ebook market share.

For the most part, print book distributors have not yet combined distribution of ebooks in their services. As a result, authors and publishers who are selling both print and digital copies of a book must have separate distribution channels for these two different formats. Ingram's Spark program (www.IngramSpark.com) is the first program to begin to offer distribution for both print and digital together.

Authors and publishers have two options in garnering distribution for their digital books: the do-it-yourself approach or an ebook distributor.

Do-It-Yourself

Since a handful of online bookstores make up the vast majority of ebook sales, it is possible for an author or publisher to submit an ebook manually to each of them. The stores listed below allows authors and publishers to publish an ebook directly to their online store via a publishing platform.

- **Amazon Kindle Direct Publishing**
  http://kdp.amazon.com

- **Apple iBookstore**
  www.apple.com/ibooks-author

- **Google eBooks**
  https://support.google.com/books/partner

- **Kobo Writing Life**
  http://www.kobo.com/writinglife

- **NookPress**
  www.nookpress.com

eBook Distributors

The best way to make sure your digital books are available to the widest range of online bookstores is to use an ebook distribution service. Some include Amazon in their distribution package, others give you the option to have them distribute to Amazon. The three main ebook distribution services for authors and small publishers are listed here.

- **BookBaby**
    BookBaby provides distribution to Amazon, iBooks, Barnes & Noble, and nine other online ebook stores.
    www.bookbaby.com

- **Ingram via Lightning Source**
    Ingram allows authors and publishers to choose whether they want to include Amazon and Apple in their ebook distribution contract.
    www.lightningsource.com

- **Smashwords**
    Smashwords provides the widest distribution of the main ebook distributors, including international bookstores and ebook subscription services. However, they do not distribute to Amazon for the majority of their titles.
    www.smashwords.com

eBook Distribution to the Christian Marketplace

As more people switch to reading digital books, revenue from the sales of print books declines. Christian bookstores have historically relied heavily on print book sales for profit. As purchasing print books over the Internet grew in popularity, Christian bookstores began to offer books for sale over the Internet as well as in their physical stores.

With the rise in popularity of digital books, Christian bookstores added ebooks to their Internet book offerings. However, these Christian bookstores do not use general market ebook distributors to place digital books in their online stores. Instead, many Christian retailers use a retail website service to maintain their online bookstores. These retail website services determine which books are listed on the retailers' website based on the distributors they use to order books. Two popular Christian retail website services are Signature Websites: Network and DeeperCalling Media.

- **Signature Websites: Network**
  Signature Websites, owned by Innovative, Inc., provides Internet bookstores solutions for over 300 Christian retail stores. These online bookstores sell ebooks as well as print books. Signature Websites: Network's website contains a complete list of the retail stores that they support.
  http://stores.signaturewebsitesnetwork.com

- **DeeperCalling Media**
  DeeperCalling provides online bookstores for about 900 Christian and secular market booksellers. These bookstores feature both print and digital books. Selling your ebooks across all of the DeeperCalling store websites is easy. Simply register an account with them, then enter your ebook title information, upload an image and your ebook files, and you are good to go.
  www.deepercalling.com

Amazon's Kindle Direct Publishing Program (KDP)

Amazon is the top source for purchasing ebooks in the United States. It is way ahead of the competition. According to data from the Book Industry Study Group (BISG), Amazon has about two-thirds of the U.S. ebook market share while its closest competitors—Barnes & Noble and then Apple—have about 10% each. Amazon is also the most lucrative ebook sales channel for publishers. A recent study found that publishers' own websites come in a distant second place for generating the most ebook sales.

Since Amazon secures most of the digital book sales in the United States, this book channel cannot be overlooked. Amazon offers a number of programs for authors and publishers selling their ebooks on the Kindle store. Authors and publishers who take advantage of these programs can increase the effectiveness of their marketing efforts.

The Kindle Owner's Lending Library: This library allows Amazon Prime member Kindle owners to check out one digital book per month with no due date, but the current book must be returned before another book is loaned. Titles can be enrolled in the Lending Library via Amazon's KDP Select program. To enroll a title in the KDP Select program, the title must be made exclusive to the Kindle Store for at least 90 days. Amazon has set aside a fund to compensate authors whose titles appear in the Lending Library. Each author's share of the monthly fund is based on an enrolled title's share of the total number of ebooks borrowed across all participating KDP titles in the Kindle Owner's Lending Library.

Amazon MatchBook: A recent study by the Book Industry Study Group (BISG) found that customers were very interested in buying "bundles"— the print and digital versions of the book together. The study indicated that bundling print and digital versions of a book together may help increase book sales. Kindle MatchBook is Amazon's bundling service. MatchBook gives Amazon customers the option to purchase the Kindle edition of print books they previously purchased or are currently purchasing from Amazon. Amazon reports that bundling has been one of its most-requested customer features. Many avid ebook readers say that they also often purchase print copies of books they really like. Kindle MatchBook gives customers the option to buy—for $2.99, $1.99, $0.99, or free—the Kindle edition of print books they have previously purchased (all the way back to 1995 when Amazon first launched its online bookstore). Authors and publishers must sign their books up for the program. Of course, to participate, a publisher must have both the print and ebook version of a book for sale via Amazon. Book bundles offered via the MatchBook program can be limited-time offers. Kindle books need not be part of KDP Select to be eligible for the MatchBook program.

Kindle Countdown Deals: These allow authors and publishers to run compelling price promotions. Kindle Countdown Deals provide readers with limited-time promotional discounts on Kindle-exclusive books. Customers can see the regular price and the promotional price on the book's detail page, as well as a countdown clock telling them how much time is left at the promotional price. Kindle Countdown Deals can be offered on any book enrolled in the KDP Select program.

Library Distribution

Public libraries all now offer their patrons the opportunity to check out ebooks. In fact, there is at least one public library in the United States that has gone all digital, no longer even offering print books. Just like the distribution channel for print books, traditional library book distributors are currently not selling ebook services to libraries. Rather, separate ebook library services fill this demand. A few of these services are listed here.

- **OverDrive**
  The number one library ebook service in the country.
  www.overdrive.com

- **ebrary**
  Provides worldwide ebook services to libraries.
  www.ebrary.com

- **Follett Digital Resources**
  This service mainly sells ebooks to school libraries.
  www.fdr.follett.com

eBook Subscription Services

For years, magazines and newspapers ruled the subscription world. Readers paid a fee to receive a daily, weekly, or monthly magazine or newspaper. The advent of digital content has revitalized the subscription business. The movie industry's largest subscription service is Netflix; the music industry's subscription services include Spotify and Rhapsody.

With consumers downloading more ebooks, music, TV shows, and movies than ever, digital content subscriptions are one of the fastest-growing e-commerce categories. It was only a matter of time before digital books would become part of a subscription trend.

The trend is still in its infancy. Currently, just three main companies offer subscription ebook services. Making your ebook available via a subscription service is another sales channel to increase revenue from your book.

- **Oyster**
  Oyster launched in September 2013 with more than 100,000 books. Their monthly subscription fee is $9.95. For this fee, users can access the books listed on the Oyster site. Oyster does not work directly with authors, but does have an agreement with Smashwords for independently published ebooks.
  www.oysterbooks.com.

- **Scribd**
  Scribd, the document sharing site, also launched a digital book subscription service in 2013. For a monthly fee of $8.99, readers can access books and other written works on their iPhone, iPad, Android device, and web browser. Scribd is the world's largest global digital library. Scribd will work with authors and publishers in acquiring ebooks for their new digital book subscription service.
  www.scribd.com

- **Entitle**
  Entitle offers a variety of subscription plans starting at $14.99. Entitle allows users to own the ebooks in their subscription, which differs from Oyster and Scribd.
  www.entitlebooks.com.

eBook Awards

With the rise of ebooks, most traditional book award programs offer at least one, if not more, categories for ebooks. In addition, a number of book awards dedicated to ebooks have emerged.

- **Digital Book Awards**
  These awards, sponsored by Digital Book World, recognize innovation, creativity, and excellence in all aspects of digital publishing.
  www.digitalbookworld.com/the-digital-book-awards

- **Epic eBook Awards**
  Sponsored by The Electronic Publishing Industry Coalition (EPIC) these awards recognize outstanding achievement in electronic publishing. Awards are given in over twenty different ebook categories.
  www.epicorg.com

- **eLit Awards**
  These awards are sponsored by the Jenkins Group, which also sponsors the Axiom Business Book Awards, the Moonbeam Awards, the Living Now Awards, and the Independent Publisher Awards. The eLit Awards honors digital titles produced in the previous year. They feature 59 different categories including religious fiction and religion.
  www.elitawards.com

- **Dan Poynter's Global eBook Awards**
  This award is sponsored by Dan Poynter (the self-publishing guru). Awards are offered in over 80 categories including some religious ones.
  http://globalebookawards.com

- **Benjamin Franklin Digital Awards**
  Sponsored by the Independent Book Publishers Association (IBPA) this award honors achievement in electronic book publishing by individuals and organizations of all sizes, including publishers, developers, designers, manufacturers, institutions, and technology leaders. The BFDA is a rolling awards program—submissions are welcomed year round and entries are judged against a standard of excellence in four categories: eBooks, Enhanced eBooks, Books as Apps, and New Technologies.
  http://bfda-ibpa.org

- **QED Seal**
  For over 100 years, the *Good Housekeeping* Seal of Approval™ has been reassuring consumers about product purchasing decisions. It is one of the most recognized consumer emblems in the market today. The *Good Housekeeping* Seal is only given to those products that the magazine has tested and approved, so that readers know that products given the seal are quality products. To reassure digital book readers that the ebook they were about to purchase is a quality product, Digital Book World has created the QED seal, basically, the equivalent of the *Good Housekeeping* Seal of Approval for ebooks.

  The QED seal (which stands for Quality, Excellence, Design) is a part of Digital Book World's Publishing Innovation Awards. The QED is designed to tell readers that the ebook title carrying the QED seal will render well in any reading format and that they can buy the ebook with confidence.

  The QED seal is judged on a thorough, professional 13-point design review with an eye towards readability across multiple devices and in multiple formats to ensure that the content renders well no matter how a reader chooses to experience it. Since the QED seal is awarded to a title, not a format, each title is judged in two formats (EPUB and Mobi), in three e-reader types, and on three screen sizes (mobile, e-ink reader, and tablet). Titles that pass the QED judging process receive the QED seal.

  Authors and publishers who want to reassure readers that their digital titles are quality ebooks—well laid out with correct formatting for a quality e-reading experience—in an effort to secure more sales can submit ebook titles for this seal of approval.
  http://qed.digitalbookworld.com

eBook Reviews

As ebooks become more integrated into the industry, more trade and consumer book review publications and websites are reviewing ebooks right along with print books. As such, many of the book review sources listed in the "Garner Book Reviews" chapter (see chapter 5) review ebooks.

One resource worth mentioning is BookRooster (www.bookrooster.com). This website is for authors (or publishers) with books in the Kindle bookstore. The site is a community of passionate readers. They organize the distribution of review copies of Kindle books for free to readers in exchange for an unbiased Amazon customer review.

Promoting Your eBooks to Readers

eBooks don't sell themselves any more than print books do. Just as publishing a print book does not guarantee sales (you must market the book to draw in consumers), so it is for making your book available in ebook format. Sales will not automatically follow. Marketing is required to drive consumers to your ebook version, just as it is with the print version.

Having one marketing strategy for both the print and ebook versions of your book can work. However, specifically marketing to ebook readers can bring in increased sales for your ebooks.

The best way to reach ebook readers is on the Internet since individuals with mobile devices tend to get the majority of their information from the World Wide Web. Below is a listing of a variety of websites where you can promote your ebook for free or a reasonable fee. While most of these websites are for the general market, religious books are accepted also.

- **Christian eBooks Today**
  This website allows authors to submit ebooks that are being offered for free. They also allow authors to submit a blog post for their website. In addition, they have advertising options for ebooks.
  www.christianebookstoday.com

- **The Vessel Project**
  This website provides a daily list of the best in free and discounted Christian ebooks, daily and weekly bestsellers, as well as notable new releases in Christian fiction and nonfiction. Some listings are free. The site also offers advertising for premium placement.
  http://vesselproject.com

- **Flurries of Words**
  This blog allows you to list Kindle books that are on special. They have a variety of options for a reasonable fee.
  http://flurriesofwords.blogspot.com

- **Digital Books Today**
  If you have a Kindle fiction ebook that has at least 25 reviews and a rating of four stars, you can promote your book on this website via an author interview, guest post, or advertise your ebook special.
  http://digitalbooktoday.com

- **Addicted to eBooks**
  If you have a Kindle ebook that is priced at $5.99 or less and has at least five reviews on Amazon, you can have your ebook listed for free on this website.
  http://addictedtoebooks.com

- **Jogena**
  This website features a directory of ebooks. Listing books is free.
  www.jogena.com

- **Indie Books List**
  This website allows you to submit an excerpt of your ebook. This site believes that the best way to promote your book is to put it in front of the reader and that the longer the excerpt, the greater the likelihood of readers becoming attached to and then buying your book. Therefore, the site requires that your excerpt be at least 1,500 words in length.
  www.indiebookslist.com

- **Only Romance**
  This website, hosted by Indie Books List, is devoted to romance novels. The site allows you to place a 1,500 word excerpt of your book with a link to where the reader can purchase the ebook.
  www.onlyromanceonline.com

Offering Free eBooks

Did you know that almost 50% of content downloaded by e-readers is free content? Offering an ebook free for a day or two is a popular way to acquire new readers and generate some buzz about your book. Another strategy some authors use is to offer a perennially free ebook to hook readers into purchasing their other titles. Whether your book is perennially free or just offered free as a promotion for a day or two, there are a number of websites that allow you to promote it to the e-reading populace.

- **Bargain eBook Hunter**
  This website allows you to submit the information about your free Kindle ebook via their contact form on their website.
  http://bargainebookhunter.com

- **FreeBooksy**
  FreeBooksy posts at least one free ebook a day. They cover multiple genres. Fill out the form on the FreeBooksy website to have your free ebook featured. This site charges a fee list your book.
  www.freebooksy.com

- **Free Kindle Books and Tips**
  If you have a free book in the Amazon Kindle store, you can submit your title to be promoted on this blog for free. Note that this site only promotes books with an average user rating of at least 4 out of 5 stars. Fill out the online form to have your book listed.
  www.fkbooksandtips.com

- **Free eBooks Daily**
  This blog features a free Kindle ebook every day.
  www.freeebooksdaily.com

- **Pixel of Ink**
  To have your free Kindle ebook promoted on this website, fill out the submission form on the site.
  www.pixelofink.com

- **Snickslist.com**
  To list your free Kindle ebook on this website, fill out the submission form on the site on the day your book is being offered for free.
  http://snickslist.com

- **That Book Place**
  This website lists free Kindle books daily. Fill out the online submission form to have your book listed. This site also features author interviews.
  www.thatbookplace.com

Digital Book Signings

The growth of digital books raises questions. How does an author sign a digital book? Are autographs even necessary for digital book lovers? It appears that digital book readers still want to collect author autographs. They do so for much the same reasons as print book readers: an autograph allows the reader to feel connected to an author and makes the book more valuable to the reader. An author can't sign a Nook, Kindle, or iPad, as doing so could potentially ruin the device (especially if he or she signed on the screen), so when it comes to digital books, how does an author sign them?

Digital autographing services allow authors to not only sign ebooks in person, they are also giving rise to digital author events. In an increasingly diverse bookselling environment, some authors are hosting digital book signings via video streaming. Such events allow authors to promote themselves and their books. After all, autographs help build relationships between authors and readers by allowing them to connect. Building relationships with readers helps to grow a writing career and sells more books.

For the majority of digital books, authors have three services to choose from to autograph digital books.

- **AuthorGraph**
  This service (originally called KindleGraph) is a free online source for authors and readers to connect. The unique service allows authors to digitally autograph an ebook and have it sent back to its original owner. Authors create a user profile on the site and upload the ASIN number of an ebook. AuthorGraph then taps into the Amazon ebook system to gather the information needed to place the book on the AuthorGraph website as available for being autographed by the author. Readers can then request a book to be signed and the author can provide a custom signature. This signature is provided via an extra page to the book that is a separate PDF version of the cover with the author's note and signature.
  www.authorgraph.com

- **Autography**
  With the Autography service, authors can sign a page that is inserted inside the front cover of an ebook, closely emulating a physical book signing. The autograph page can include custom graphics or even a photograph with the reader if they meet at an event. Autography supports all major ebook formats. With the Autography service, the author autograph can be done before or after the purchase of the ebook. This service charges fees.
  www.autography.com

- **MyWrite**
  MyWrite enables authors to sell personalized, autographed, digital copies of their book at point of sale. By using a tablet device (iPad or iPhone) and connecting to the MyWrite service, authors can insert a personalized autograph into an ebook, and then send the reader their custom copy via email in seconds. MyWrite charges a flat, yearly subscription fee per ebook title.
  www.mywrite.com

The Physical Selling of Digital Books

Strike while the iron is hot. Close the deal. A bird in the hand is worth two in the bush. These sales clichés and others like them speak to the importance of making the sale. Most people know that the best way to make a sale is to do it immediately while the customer is in your presence showing interest. This is difficult to do with digital books. As the trend moves toward purchasing and buying more digital books, the question arises: How does an author sell digital books in person?

eBook cards are one great solution to promoting and selling ebooks at events, author signings, conferences, and even bookstores to increase readership and grow sales. Understanding this need for authors to be able to sell digital books in the physical realm so they don't lose out on potential sales, two new companies, Livrada and Enthrill, have come up with an interesting solution.

- **Livrada**
  Livrada allows authors (and publishers) to purchase wallet-sized (or larger) cards featuring an ebook on the front and a unique pin

number on the back to download a digital version (EPUB or Kindle) of the book.

http://livrada.com

- **Enthrill**
  Enthrill offers a way for authors to sell their ebooks in person. Unlike Livrada, Enthrill hosts the ebooks on their site. The ebooks can be downloaded to all e-reading devices. All that is required for readers to download ebooks from Enthrill is an email address and a unique 12-digit redemption code. Authors can have their own cards printed by any printer, using the codes purchased from Enthrill, and then use these cards to sell ebooks in person.

  http://entrill.com

Creative Marketing

Finding readers in a crowded market is a challenge. As the ebook market has become increasingly crowded due to the low cost of producing an ebook, getting people to notice your book has become increasingly difficult. Here is where a little creative marketing comes in. Think outside the box. Consider interesting and unique ways to promote your ebook.

One idea is to piggy-back on existing promotions to encourage readers to buy and read your ebooks. Every March, a week is dedicated to promoting ebooks. This week, called "Read an eBook Week," has been promoting ebook reading for a decade. It has become so popular, that now the whole month of March is "Read an eBook Month." The site promoting this special week and month offers free banners to place on websites, blogs, and social media sites. Anyone offering a free ebook for the "Read an eBook Week" gets a listing on the website. You can find out more about this calendar event and how to use it to help promote your ebooks at www.ebookweek.com.

Summary

As ebook reading grows, the types of ebooks and the number of services selling digital books in creative ways will grow. There are already websites offering ebooks for free, but these free ebooks come with ads. Other websites offer readers the ability to pay only for the portion of the ebook they read so they don't waste their money if they decide they don't like the book.

— Sarah Bolme —

This chapter did not even touch on enhanced ebooks, however this format of digital books is quickly becoming popular.

Whether ebooks will overtake print books is not the important issue. The important thing to remember is that books do not sell themselves. Just like print books, ebooks must be marketed to readers to garner awareness and sales. As the number of ebooks continues to grow, publishers and authors will have to continue to find creative ways to grab readers' attention.

The Homeschool Market

*Train a child in the way he should go,
and when he is old he will not turn from it.*
—Proverbs 22:6

> Marketing Fundamental:
> **People with an emotional investment
> make more purchases.**

Homeschooling is a growing phenomenon. From 1999 to 2013, the number of children who were homeschooled increased by 75%. The number of children whose parents choose to educate them at home rather than a traditional academic setting is growing seven times faster than the number of new children enrolling in traditional K-12 schools every year. The U.S. Department of Education's National Center for Education Statistics (NCES) reports that from 2008 to 2013, homeschooling grew 17%. Currently, 1,770,000 students are homeschooled in the United States, representing 3.4% of the school-age population.

This growth in homeschooling has spurred an estimated $1.5 billion annual market supplying parents with teaching materials and lesson aids. The National Center for Education Statistics (NCES) reports that the average homeschool family spends $600 per child per year on educational resources.

Since 1999, the number of homeschooled children has increased 75%.

While it is difficult to find statistics citing how many of these homeschoolers are "Christian," it is generally believed that Christians make up the majority of the homeschool market. In one recent study, 77% of parents said they homeschooled because of a desire to provide moral instruction.

Even if your book is not specifically geared toward homeschoolers but is geared toward youth or parents, consider including this growing group in your marketing plans and efforts. As with any product, the key to selling in the homeschool market is gaining the attention of your target audience. A growing number of avenues are available to promote and sell your products in the Christian homeschool marketplace.

Homeschool Associations

Important issues for families who homeschool are support, encouragement, and the protected right to home educate their children freely. Every state hosts at least one homeschool association that works to protect the right to home educate and helps homeschool families network with each other for support. Some states have multiple associations. Homeschool associations generally provide their members with a regular newsletter. Publishers can use these newsletters to inform homeschoolers about their products. Some homeschool associations allow advertising in their newsletters while others allow article submissions featuring an author byline through which products can be promoted.

Practical Homeschooling provides a comprehensive list of homeschool associations by state with a link to each organization's website. This list can be found online at www.home-school.com/groups.

While most homeschool associations serve specific states, a few nationwide homeschool associations exist that service special populations.

- **National Challenged Homeschoolers Associated Network**
  This network is for Christian families homeschooling special needs children.
  www.nathhan.com

- **National Black Home Educators (NBHE)**
  NBHE is a resource network founded to encourage, support and offer fellowship to Black families who are home educating. Among other things, they host an annual conference and a book club.
  www.nbhe.net

- **Homeschooling Catholic**
  This group is for Catholic homeschoolers and provides links to the Catholic homeschooling conventions around the country.
  www.homeschoolingcatholic.com

Distribution

To sell to this group, you must get your books in front of them. More importantly, get your books in the channels that this group trusts and buys from to succeed in selling to homeschoolers.

Christian Retail Stores

With the growth of homeschooling, CBA encourages their members to include a homeschool section in their stores. CBA sees this as one way for Christian retail stores to reinvent themselves to remain viable in the bookstore marketplace. Most of the Christian wholesale book companies carry some homeschool materials. However, Send The Light distribution has positioned itself as the homeschool material source for Christian retail stores. Send The Light's Homeschool Store website lists, by state, Christian retail stores that sell homeschool materials.

- **Send The Light, Inc.**
  Homeschool Headquarters
  100 Biblica Way
  Elizabethton, TN 37643
  Contact: Lisa Bowman
  lisa.bowman@stl-distribution.com
  800-289-2772
  www.homeschoolstore.com

Homeschool Mail-Order Catalogs

Many homeschool families order from homeschool catalogs when purchasing materials. Numerous homeschool catalogs are available in the Christian homeschool market. Many publishers of homeschool materials produce catalogs showcasing their products and include products from other publishers. Placement of your book in a Christian homeschool catalog helps increase exposure for your title in this growing marketplace.

Each catalog company has its own process for considering materials for inclusion in its product catalog. Contact each catalog company to acquire their submission guidelines and to ensure that they are accepting materials. These catalog companies also host online bookstores, so getting your book into their catalog also ensures your book is available in their online store.

A few of the larger Christian homeschool catalogs are mentioned here.

- **Christian Book Distributors (CBD)**
  Homeschool Catalog
  140 Summit Street
  Peabody, MA 01960
  www.christianbook.com

- **HomeschoolingBooks.com**
  A Mott Media Company
  1130 Fenway Circle
  Fenton, MI 48430
  866-473-0737
  www.homeschoolingbooks.com

- **Love to Learn**
  741 North State Rd. 198
  Salem, UT 84653
  801-423-2009
  www.lovetolearn.net

- **My Father's World**
  PO Box 2140
  Rolla, MO 65402
  573-202-2000
  info@mfwbooks.com
  www.mfwbooks.com

- **Queen Homeschool Supply**
  168 Plantz Ridge Rd.
  New Freeport, PA 15352
  888-695-2777
  sandi@queenhomeschool.com
  www.queenhomeschool.com

- **Rainbow Resource Center**
  655 Township Road 500E
  Toulon, IL 61483
  888-841-3456
  info@rainbowresource.com
  http://rainbowresource.com

- **Sonlight Catalog**
  Sonlight Curriculum, Ltd.
  8042 South Grant Way
  Littleton, CO 80122
  303-730-6292
  www.sonlight.com

- **Timberdoodle Company**
  1510 E Spencer Lake Rd.
  Shelton, WA 98584
  800-478-0672
  mailbag@timberdoodle.com
  www.timberdoodle.com

Online Homeschool Bookstores

Every mail-order catalog company features an online store in addition to their snail-mail catalog. However, there are many more websites selling books and curricula. These websites do not have mail-order catalogs but rely on word of mouth and advertising to acquire customers and make sales. Each of these websites offers publishers and authors another avenue for selling books.

The main homeschool online bookstores are listed on the following page.

- **Books on the Path**
  208-762-3939
  service@booksonthepath.com
  www.booksonthepath.com

- **Children's Books, Inc.**
  800-344-3198
  ChildrensBooks@earthlink.net
  www.homeschooldiscountproducts.com

- **Hearts at Home Curriculum Store**
  3131F East 29th Street
  Bryan, TX 77802
  979-209-0782
  www.heartsathomestore.com

- **Home Educator's Resource**
  410 E Church St.
  Lewisville, TX 75067
  972-956-8320
  www.homeeducatorsresource.com

- **Homeschooling Supply**
  info@homeschoolingsupply.com
  www.homeschoolingsupply.com

- **HomesSchoolSuperCenter.com**
  888-689-4626
  www.homeschoolsupercenter.com

Homeschool eBooks

Many homeschoolers are technologically savvy and purchase ebooks for curricula or supplemental material. Publishers producing ebooks for the homeschool market should consider finding affiliate homeschool websites to promote your ebooks.

In addition to selling ebooks on your website, offer your ebooks through general market ebook stores and those geared toward the homeschool marketplace. Generally, ebook stores will list your ebook for free and pay you a percentage of each sale. The largest website selling homeschool digital material is:

- **CurrClick**
  www.currclick.com

Homeschool Magazines

One good way to reach a large segment of the homeschooling population is through magazines for homeschoolers. These magazines offer a variety of ways for publishers and authors to promote their products.

Advertising in homeschool magazines is one way to place your product before homeschoolers on a regular basis. Another is to write articles for these magazines. Writing articles for or placing excerpts from your latest titles in homeschool magazines can grab homeschoolers' attention and increase your book sales.

Homeschool magazines also provide product reviews for their readers. Some accept products directly and generate their own reviews, while others only accept review articles from homeschoolers who have used a product and approve of it. Many homeschool magazines post product reviews on their websites and feature them in their e-zines along with their print magazine.

Homeschool families rely on these reviews when considering new or supplementary material for their individual homeschool programs. Unlike most publications that provide reviews, many homeschooling magazines do not require that a product be brand new. As long as a product is newer, or even just new to the homeschool market, these publications are willing to consider a review.

As with any review, it is best to contact the editor of each publication before submitting your products. This allows editors to provide information and instructions on how they want products submitted and keeps you, the publisher, from wasting time and money sending out materials to magazines that will not review your book.

Following are five major national publications that reach the Christian homeschool market:

- **Home Educating Family Magazine**
  http://hedua.com/magazine

- **Homeschool Enrichment Magazine**
  Homeschool Enrichment, Inc.
  PO Box 163
  Pekin, IL 61555
  800-558-9523
  www.homeschoolenrichment.com

- **Homeschooling Today Magazine**
  PO Box 1092
  Somerset, KY 42502
  606-485-4105
  www.homeschooltoday.com

- **Practical Homeschooling**
  Home Life, Inc.
  PO Box 1190
  Fenton, MO 63026-1190
  636-343-6786
  www.home-school.com

- **The Homeschool Digest**
  Wisdom's Gate
  PO Box 374
  Covert, MI 49043
  269-764-1910
  editor@wisgate.com
  www.homeschooldigest.com

- **The Old Schoolhouse Magazine**
  PO Box 8426
  Gray, TN 37615
  888-718-HOME
  Publishers@TheHomeschoolMagazine.com
  www.thehomeschoolmagazine.com

Reaching Homeschoolers on the Internet

Many homeschoolers use technology on a daily basis in teaching their children. Hence, most are comfortable on the Internet and use it to access information, support, and teaching resources. Using the Internet to reach Homeschoolers with your books is about meeting up with homeschoolers where they are already hanging out.

Christian Homeschool Websites

Many homeschool families seek support through the Internet. As a result, a fair number of Christian homeschool support websites exist. These multipurpose sites feature information, chat rooms, message boards, helpful links, and reviews of products. Many also sell homeschool products on their website.

Homeschool support websites offer many opportunities for publishers and authors to promote books. Publishers and authors can submit books for review, join the discussion groups, write articles for the website or its e-newsletter, advertise on the website or in the site's e-newsletter, and become an affiliate. Some of these homeschool support websites receive over 4,000 visitors a day.

A few of the larger Christian homeschooling websites are listed here.

- **A to Z Home's Cool**
  http://a2zhomeschooling.com/

- **Eclectic Homeschool Online**
  http://eclectichomeschool.org

- **EHO Lite: Beginning Homeschooling**
  www.eho.org

- **Home Educators Resource Directory**
  www.homeeddirectory.com

- **Home School, Inc.**
  www.home-school-inc.com
  www.homeschoolreviews.com

- **Homeschool.com**
  www.homeschool.com

— Sarah Bolme —

- **HomeschoolBuzz.com**
  http://homeschoolbuzz.com

- **HomeschoolChristian.com**
  www.homeschoolchristian.com

- **Homeschooling From the Heart**
  www.homeschoolingfromtheheart.com

Homeschool Blogs

Blogs are another means to reach large numbers of homeschoolers. As a publisher or author, you can create your own homeschool blog and you can guest post and advertise on others' homeschool blogs to increase exposure of your products within the homeschool community. Many homeschoolers also do reviews of products on their blogs, so finding homeschool blogs to review your product can provide a boost to your sales. One good place to find a listing of homeschool bloggers is on Homeschool Blogging at http://homeschoolblogging.com/find-a-blogger.

Planning and setting up your own homeschool blog review tour can be time consuming. *The Old Schoolhouse Magazine* runs a blog review service. They have a blog review crew composed of around 250 homeschool families that love to blog about homeschool products. For a fee you can have a book or product reviewed on up to 100 homeschool blogs. To learn more about this program, visit http://schoolhousereviewcrew.com.

Homeschool Radio Programs

Since homeschooling is still a niche community, radio programs for homeschoolers are typically broadcast over the Internet. Most of these radio programs interview guests that can make a contribution to meeting the needs of homeschoolers. Authors with books on subjects of interest to homeschoolers would fall into this category. Radio can be a great way to connect with homeschoolers to inform them of your books. The Ultimate Homeschool Radio Network (http://ultimateradioshow.com) is a site comprised of various show hosts with a heart for home school families. It is a great place to find numerous radio shows geared for the homeschool market looking for guests.

Homeschool e-Newsletters

A number of publishers that produce materials for the Christian homeschool market also produce e-newsletters. e-Newsletters provide these publishers a way to connect regularly with previous and potential customers. Each newsletter provides the consumer with valuable information and directs them back to the publisher's products. Many publishers send their e-newsletter automatically to anyone who purchases a product, and they also include a way for visitors to sign up for the free e-newsletter on their website.

Producing an e-newsletter can be time consuming and building a consumer base to send your newsletter to takes even more time. If you are a publisher with only one or two titles for the homeschool marketplace, consider piggybacking on existing e-newsletters to advertise your products. Many e-newsletters include paid advertisements and some will include articles from authors looking to promote their products.

The average homeschool family spends $600 per child per year on educational resources.

While no central registry of homeschool e-newsletters exists, one good place to start is with the large homeschool websites. Many of them produce regular newsletters for their audience. For example, The Home Educators Resource Director (www.homeeddirectory.com) and Homeschool.com (www.homeschool.com) both produce monthly newsletters.

In addition, a number of publishers publishing curriculum for the Christian homeschool market produce e-newsletters with substantial circulations. You can find publishers with newsletters through the discussion groups that focus on marketing to the homeschool market. These include the Christian Self-Publishing group on Yahoo and the Christian Homeschooling Publishing and Marketing group on Facebook (see chapter 1).

Homeschool Conventions

A few hundred homeschool conventions are held across the United States each year. Homeschool conventions provide publishers of homeschool materials a good venue for placing products in front of homeschoolers.

Homeschool conventions feature seminars for homeschool parents to acquire new and innovative ideas for teaching their children. They also include exhibit halls with homeschool materials for attendees to browse and purchase. Most conferences produce handouts for attendees, which contain advertising materials for homeschool products.

As homeschooling has grown, so have the services for homeschoolers. While many of homeschool conventions are put on by state homeschool associations, the number of organizations hosting homeschool conventions around the country is growing. A few of these homeschool convention organizations include:

- **American Homes Education and Discipleship (AHEAD)**
  http://americanhomeeducation.org

- **Great Homeschool Conventions**
  www.greathomeschoolconventions.com

- **Teach Them Diligently**
  https://teachthemdiligently.net

Another resource for a listing of homeschool conventions is provided by *Practical Homeschooling* on their website. This list can be found at www.home-school.com/events. A listing of homeschool conventions in Canada can be found at www.joycenter.on.ca/confer.htm.

Speaking at Homeschool Conventions

Publishers who want to include speaking and exhibiting at homeschool conventions in their marketing plan should consider joining the Homeschool Speakers and Vendors Association (HSVA).

HSVA (www.homeschoolvendors.org) provides its members with unlimited access to a complete database of homeschool conventions. They also host a Convention Speakers Bureau that lists individuals who provide presentations at homeschool conventions. Homeschool convention planners can browse this list to find speakers for their events.

The Old Schoolhouse Magazine hosts a homeschool convention Speakers Bureau. Their intent is to offer homeschool convention planners and homeschool associations a pool of speakers from which to choose for conventions and other homeschool events. Listing in this homeschool speakers bureau is free. The Old Schoolhouse Speakers Bureau can be found at www.homeschoolspeakers.com.

Homeschool Convention Bags

An affordable alternative to exhibiting materials at homeschool conventions is to participate in a convention bag-stuffing program. Homeschool conventions generally give attendees bags filled with promotional materials for homeschool products. Publishers can place marketing materials in homeschool convention attendee bags as an alternative or in addition to exhibiting at a convention.

The homeschool convention market has a convention bag stuffing service run by Great Stuff Convention Bags, Inc. This service provides convention bags for over 150 homeschool conventions each year, providing more than 100,000 bags to conference attendees. Publishers can choose the conventions at which they want to make their materials available. Great Stuff Convention Bags then places the promotional materials in convention bags for a fee and delivers them to the homeschool conventions.

- **Great Stuff Convention Bags, Inc.**
    www.greatstuffconventionbags.com

Online Homeschool Conventions

A couple companies run online homeschool conventions. These conventions feature all the aspects of a physical homeschool convention, but with everything provided online. Specializing in reaching rural families, missionary families in foreign countries, and those who cannot attend a regular homeschool convention, these online homeschool conventions provide authors and publishers another way to reach the homeschool market.

- **The Homeschool Conference**
    This annual conference is a two-day, online, free worldwide event.
    www.homeschoolconference.com

- **Schoolhouse Expo**
    Run by *The Old Schoolhouse Magazine*, the Schoolhouse Expo hosts an annual online convention.
    http://schoolhouseexpo.com

- **Ultimate Homeschool Expo**
    Run by Media Angels, this online expo provides a wide variety of speakers who address a number of topics for today's homeschool moms. The Expo hosts both live and on-demand events.
    www.mediaangels.com/expo

Homeschool Direct Mailings

Card packs offer an affordable marketing strategy to reach the Christian homeschool market. Card packs are stacks of promotional cards from a variety of vendors bundled together in a plastic wrap package and mailed to a list of target consumers. This type of direct mail advertising is more cost effective than solo direct mail. Most card pack companies provide some design services for your postcard insert promoting your products. The main company providing affordable card pack direct mailing to homeschoolers is Tri-Media Marketing Services (www.trimediaonline.com). They also offer rental of mailing lists of homeschoolers for those who want to conduct their own mailing. In addition, you can rent the company's email list of homeschool families for an email blast.

Summary

As the homeschool market continues to grow, the need for quality materials for this group will continue to increase. The opportunities for marketing in this growing marketplace are increasing and changing each year.

18

The Urban Market

*I have other sheep that are not of this sheep pen.
I must bring them also. They too will listen to my voice,
and there shall be one flock and one shepherd.*
—John 10:16

> Marketing Fundamental:
> **People trust the recommendations
> of their family and friends.**

African-American publishers and authors can effectively reach the Christian market using all the resources listed in previous chapters of this book. However, there are a number of resources that target the Urban Christian market specifically. This chapter is dedicated to those resources.

The Urban Christian market is the market that reaches African-Americans. The most recent census estimates that African-Americans make up about 13% of the population of the United States. This group tends to be very religious, holding a strong belief in God. African-American church attendance is

50% higher than the general population. The Barna Research group reports that African-Americans are the strongest per capita religious consumers in America. This means that this group purchases religious products at a higher rate than the remainder of the population of the United States.

February is African-American History Month. This celebration, founded in 1926 by Dr. Carter G. Woodson as Negro History Week, eventually grew to a month in 1976 when President Gerald R. Ford urged Americans to honor the accomplishments of Black Americans in every area of endeavor. February provides authors with many bonus opportunities for promoting their books.

Urban Christian Distribution

Urban Christian booksellers generally order their books through the established Christian distribution channel (chapter 3). One company, Black Christian Book Company, LLC (www.blackchristianbookcompany.com) grew out of the need for Black authors and books geared for the Urban Christian market to have better representation in general Christian bookstores. This company offers an online bookstore featuring books written by Black authors.

Urban Book Reviews

A few publications geared toward the Urban book reader offer reviews of books. These publications are general market focused, but do offer reviews of Christian-themed books.

- **African American Literature Book Club (AALBC)**
  AALBC is the largest and most frequently visited website dedicated to books by and about black people. Their mission is to promote the diverse spectrum of literature written for, or about, people of African descent by helping readers find the books and authors they will enjoy. The site reviews books for a fee.
  www.aalbc.com

- **QBR: The Black Book Review**
  This review publication is an online magazine that allows readers to post reviews of books for and about the African-American experience for free. The site provides advertising opportunities. They also host the Harlem Book Fair each year.

QBR: *The Black Book Review*
591 Warburton Avenue #170
Hastings on Hudson, NY 10706
914-231-6778
reviews@qbr.com
www.qbr.com

- **RAWSISTAZ Literary Group**
The RAWSISTAZ is an online reading group for women aged 17 and up with a desire to discuss and share information of importance to the literary community. They do book reviews, which they host on their review website at www.blackbookreviews.net.
RAWSISTAZ Literary Group
attn: Reviews Editor
5885 Cumming Hwy., Ste 108-232
Sugar Hill, GA 30518
www.rawsistaz.com

- *Shades of Romance Magazine*
This quarterly online publication features interviews, book reviews, and articles of multicultural novels. The magazine features eight authors each issue.
Shades of Romance Magazine
attn: LaShaunda C. Hoffman, Editor
7127 Minnesota Ave.
St. Louis, MO 63111
sorgmag@yahoo.com
www.sormag.com

- *Black Pearls Magazine*
Black Pearls Magazine is a biweekly, free online magazine written to inspire readers. They also host the Black Authors Network Radio Show (www.blogtalkradio.com/black-author-network). While they do not do book reviews, they accept submissions of articles featuring reviews of books. Advertising is also available.
http://blackpearlsmagazine.com

- **All the Buzz Literary Reviews**
  Featuring reviews, excerpts, and interviews, All the Buzz is an online site for African-American literature. The site also provides a virtual book tour service.
  http://allthebuzzreviews.com

Urban Press Release Services

Authors and publishers can also use press releases service to target African-American Christian consumers, church leaders, and media outlets. There are a number of press release and email blast services aimed directly at the Urban Christian market. These services charge a fee to send your press release or email blast to thousands of recipients.

- **Black Book Promo**
  www.blackbookpromo.com

- **Black Christian Book Promo**
  http://blackchristianbookpromo.com

- **BlackPR.com**
  www.blackpr.com

- **Gospel EBlast**
  www.gospeleblast.com

- **Vision Christian Newswire**
  http://visionchristiannewswire.com

Getting your press release in Urban print and online media is a great way to reach Urban consumers. A good way to get your news story into Black newspapers is to utilize the services newspaper associations offer.

- **The National Newspaper Publishers Association (NNPA)**
  NNPA is a trade association for more than 200 Black community newspapers across the nation. The organization hosts a convention. Advertising options to reach the 200+ newspapers are also available.

The association hosts the BlackPressUSA (www.blackpressusa.com) website, which serves as an online community for Black newspapers.
NNPA
1816 12th Street, NW
Washington, DC 20009
202-588-8764
info@nnpa.org
www.nnpa.org

Another way to reach the Black media is through targeting Black journalists. Using an organization like the National Association of Black Journalists can be an effective way to reach these professionals.

- **National Association of Black Journalists (NABJ)**
  This is a membership-based organization for Black journalists. The organization produces a quarterly journal for their members, hosts a national conference annually, grants journalistic awards, and provides contact information for African-American media and other organizations for journalists of color.
  NABJ
  1100 Knight Hall, Suite 3100
  College Park, Maryland 20742
  301-405-0248
  www.nabj.org

Urban Christian Speakers Bureaus

Authors looking to launch a speaking tour or ministry to the African-American community can promote themselves through speakers bureaus aimed at this market.

- **BlackExperts.com**
  BlackExperts.com is a unique online directory that allows African American experts to profile themselves in front of journalists and television and radio producers. This service is a directory rather than a speakers bureau because it is geared toward journalists needing sources for information and interviews.
  www.blackexperts.com

- **BlackSpeakers.com**
  BlackSpeakers.com, a sister site to BlackExperts.com, is an online directory that allows meeting planners seeking African-American speakers for events to locate presenters. They have a flat fee that places each listing on both websites.
  www.blackspeakers.com

- **Gospel Interviews**
  Hosted by Larry W. Robinson, this website features musical reviews of Black artists and interviews of Black authors.
  www.gospelinterviews.com

Urban Christian Reading Groups

Reading groups for African-American readers are very popular. Marketing to reading groups has become a hot trend in bookselling (see chapter 12 for how to use reading groups to promote your books). There are a number of websites that promote and support African-American reading groups.

- **Mosaic Books**
  Mosaic Books boasts the largest list of African-American book clubs available on the Internet. This website allows you to search by state to find reading groups and provides contact information. The website also allows self-publishers and small presses to promote their books on the Mosaic Books website for a fee.
  www.mosaicbooks.com.

- **RAWSISTAZ Literary Group**
  RAWSISTAZ is an online reading group for women ages 17 and up with a desire to discuss and share information of importance to the literary community.
  www.rawsistaz.com

- **The Good Girl Book Club**
  This book club is reorganizing and plans to re-launch their program in 2014. They have a Publisher's Book Promotion Program to help authors and publishers reach thousands of avid readers.
  www.goodgirlbookclubonline.com

Urban Christian Book Clubs

Two book clubs offering books for African-American readers are available for publishers to pursue. Book clubs typically purchase books at a heavily discounted rate from publishers and then sell these books to their members. Getting a book in a book club is usually a great opportunity for publishers as it exposes thousands of readers to your book.

- **Black Expressions**
  This is a general market book club run by the same people who own Doubleday Book Club, Children's Book-of-the-Month Club, Crossings Book Club, and many others. They also feature Christian titles.
  www.blackexpressions.com

- **Black Inspirations Book Club**
  Black Inspirations is a smaller book club that only sells books that glorify God.
  www.bicbc.com

Urban Radio and Television

Many African-American broadcasting networks exist across the United States. Authors who wish to be guests on Urban radio and television will have the best success in securing appearances through hiring a publicist familiar with this market. However, if you are on a limited budget and want the do-it-yourself method, there are some resources available to put you in touch with the Black media.

- **Black Entertainment Television (BET)**
  This television network is devoted to the African-American viewer. BET reaches over 40 million cable households.
  www.bet.com

- **National Association of Black Owned Broadcasters (NABOB)**
  NABOB is the first and largest trade organization representing the interests of African-American owners of radio and television stations across the country. They host an annual convention and provide a listing of their members by state on their website.
  www.nabob.org

- **Preach The Word Worldwide Network**
  Preach The Word Worldwide Network TV is a 24/7 Christian television network reaching homes around the world. They offer opportunities for hosting a television show as well as advertising.
  www.ptwwntv.com

African-American Church Denominations

One resourceful way to reach African-American church leaders and attendees is through one of the predominately African-American church denominations. These groups hold all types of conferences for their leaders and laypeople. Promoting your book through one of these conferences, being a speaker at a conference, or just using the denominational contacts to get a great endorsement for your book are all ways authors and publishers can tap into African-American church denominations to maximize your marketing efforts. The larger African-American church denominations are listed here.

- **African Methodist Episcopal Church (AME)**
  www.ame-church.com

- **African Methodist Episcopal Zion Church (AME Zion)**
  www.amez.org

- **Church of God in Christ**
  www.cogic.com

- **National Baptist Convention, USA, Inc.**
  www.nationalbaptist.com

Historically Black Colleges and Universities

Historically Black Colleges and Universities (HBCU) were founded in the late 1800s to address the educational needs of freed slaves and Native Americans. These colleges and universities are today's top producers of professional African-American talent. For publishers and authors seeking to market books to African-American professors and students of higher education, these colleges and universities are your target.

A few websites host listings of Historically Black Colleges and Universities in the United States. These listings can be found at www.hbcupages.com and www.edonline.com/cq/hbcu/alphabet.htm. For those seeking to target the HBCU library market, the HBCU Library Alliance lists contact information for their member college and university libraries by state on their website at http://hbculibraries.org/html/memberlibraries-state.html.

African-American Homeschoolers

Conservative figures estimate that African Americans make up five to ten percent of the homeschooling population. Researchers say the number of black parents who are homeschooling may be the fastest-growing segment of American homeschooling. A few resources are available for publishers and authors to market their books to this portion of the homeschooling population.

- **National Black Home Educations (NBHE)**
  The National Black Home Educators (NBHE) is a resource network founded to encourage, support and offer fellowship to families who are home educating. Among other things, they host an annual conference and a book club.
  www.nbhe.net

Urban Book Awards

Many book award programs offer African-American categories. A few general book awards specifically commend and promote books by African-American authors. These Urban book awards offer religious categories or accept religious books for the categories they sponsor awards in.

- **African-American Literary Awards Show**
  This annual award was started to bring recognition to African-American authors throughout the country. It is the most comprehensive awards show to recognize, honor, celebrate, and promote the outstanding achievements and contributions that authors and writers make to the publishing, arts, and entertainment industries.
  www.literaryawardshow.com

- **BCALA Literary Awards**
    The Black Caucus of the American Library Association (BCALA) hosts this annual award to honor books written by African-American authors. The award is offered in three categories: First Novelist, Fiction, and Nonfiction.
    www.bcala.org/awards/literary.htm

- **The Hurston/Wright Legacy Award™**
    This award, given by The Hurston/Wright Foundation, is the first national award presented to published writers of African descent by the national community of Black writers. The award is offered for four categories and nominations must be submitted by the publisher with permission from the author.
    www.hurstonwright.org

Social Networking for Urban Authors

African-American Christian authors have a great resource for connecting with and networking with other Christian authors and industry professional on a social network site developed just for this purpose.

ChocolatePagesNetwork.com allows authors to interact and connect with other authors to share interests and experiences while building their database of professional contacts to help expand their marketing efforts. This network can be found online at www.chocolatepagesonline.com.

Summary

African-American authors and those publishers publishing African-American authors have both the general Christian market channels as well as the Urban Christian market channels available for promoting their books. When harnessed effectively, this increased marketing potential can produce fruitful results.

19

Spanish-Language Books

*After this I looked and there before me was a great multitude
that no one could count, from every nation, tribe,
people, and language, standing before the
throne and in front of the Lamb.*
—Revelation 7:9

> Marketing Fundamental:
> **Offering language choices brings more customers.**

Hispanics are the largest and fastest-growing minority group in the United States. The most recent census shows this group accounts for one out of every six U.S. residents. Eight states in the U.S. have one million or more Hispanic residents: Arizona, California, Colorado, Florida, Illinois, New Jersey, New York, and Texas. In addition, the average Hispanic family income is increasing, making this population group's buying power increase. Hispanic buying power is expected to grow another 50% over the next five years.

Spanish is the third most common language in the world. With the continued Hispanic population increase in the United States, Spanish-language products are growing and selling well. The U.S. Hispanic book buying market is estimated at about $1 billion, of which 30 to 35 percent comes from Spanish language books.

Sales of Spanish-language Christian titles have continued to increase each year for the past decade. Self-help and spiritual books are the biggest sellers among Hispanics. The Spanish titles that are the biggest sellers in the Hispanic Christian book market are almost all translations of English-language books.

In 2003, the Association of American Publishers (AAP) named June Latino Book Month to promote books for and by Latinos. Since that time, trade shows and book fairs for this language group have increased dramatically.

Spanish-Language Products Association

Due to the growth of Spanish-language Christian products, many large Christian publishing houses have added Spanish-language divisions. The Spanish Evangelical Products Association (SEPA), a publishers' association, was formed to serve the growing number of Christian publishers producing Spanish-language materials.

- **Spanish Evangelical Products Association (SEPA)**
  1360 NW 88 Ave.
  Miami, FL 33172
  305-503-1195
  www.sepaweb.org

Spanish-Language Trade Shows

Spanish Christian product shows present an opportunity for publishers to display Spanish-language titles to the Christian Spanish-speaking retail marketplace.

- **Expolit**
  This Hispanic Christian products trade show is held in Florida each year.
  www.expolit.com

- **Expo Cristiana**
  This Spanish-language Christian products trade show is held annually in Mexico City.
  www.expocristiana.com

- **Latino Book and Family Festival**
  Hosted by Latino Literacy Now, this is a traveling book show for the general Hispanic market. Each year they hold festivals in California and Chicago. These festivals feature exhibitors and speakers.
  www.lbff.us

- **LéaLA**
  LéaLA is a Hispanic book fair in Los Angeles for the general population.
  www.lea-la.com/en/

Spanish-Language Book Reviews

Many industry trade publications, including *Publishers Weekly* and *Library Journal*, provide reviews of Spanish-language books either in each edition of their magazine or in special Spanish-language editions. One Christian retail publication offers reviews of Christian Spanish-language products:

- *Christian Retailing*
  This magazine for Christian retailers has a section of each edition devoted to news and reviews of Spanish-language titles.
  407-333-0600
  Chris Johnson
  chris.johnson@charismamedia.com
  www.christianretailing.com

Spanish-Language Distribution

The major Christian book distributors and wholesale book companies (see chapter 3) all stock and sell Spanish-language titles as many Christian retail stores include a Spanish-language section as part of their store offerings. However, reaching exclusively Spanish-language Christian stores takes a little more effort. A couple distributors exclusively devoted to Spanish-language products are:

- **Lectorum**
  This company is the nation's biggest and oldest Spanish-language book distributor. They sell to schools, libraries, and bookstores throughout the United States.
  800-345-5946
  www.lectorum.com

- **Spanish Book Distributor, Inc. (SBD)**
  SBD is a distributor specialized on bringing the newest books in the Spanish language to the U.S. market and abroad.
  800-609-2113
  www.sbdbooks.com

Big-box retailers such as Walmart®, Costco®, and Sam's Club® are increasingly selling Spanish-language products, including Christian titles. The following distributors specialize in the distribution of Spanish-language books to these large general-market retailers.

- **Anderson Merchandisers**
  This company sells to Walmart and Sam's Club.
  800-894-2780
  www.amerch.com

- **ReaderLink Distribution Services, LLC**
  ReaderLink is the largest full-service distributor of hardcover, trade, and paperback books to non-trade channel booksellers in North America, including the biggest names in retail across multiple retail channels.
  800-549-5389
  www.readerlink.com

Spanish-Language Radio and Television

Authors seeking to be media guests on Spanish-language radio and television must speak fluent Spanish (unless you are being interviewed for an English station that also broadcasts in Spanish). Many Spanish radio and television stations broadcast to Central and South America as well as North America. When looking to find Spanish stations to query for guest appearances, a few options are available for authors and publishers.

- **3ABN Latino**
  This organization is a Spanish-language satellite television and radio network.
  www.3abnlatino.org

- **Radio Cristiana**
  Operated by Christian Vision USA, Inc., this Spanish-language Christian radio broadcast has a large international reach by satellite.
  http://cvclavoz.com

- **Enlace**
  Enlace is radio program with an international reach via satellite communication.
  www.enlace.org

- **Christian Television Network International (CTN)**
  CTN is broadcast out of Florida to the United States, Canada, Central and South America, and parts of Europe.
  www.ctni.org

- **Club 700 Hoy**
  Club 700 Hoy is the Spanish-language 700 Club program.
  www.club700hoy.com

- **Catholic Radio and Television Network (CRTN)**
  This network provides a listing of Catholic radio stations in North and South America, including Spanish-language radio stations, with links to each station's website.
  www.crtn.org

- **Radio-Locator**
  This website features a radio station search engine that includes Spanish-language radio stations in the United States as well as worldwide radio stations.
  www.radio-locator.com

Press Releases

Authors and publishers can use press release services to target Hispanic radio, television, and other media outlets. Companies that offer Hispanic newswire services are geared toward the general Hispanic marketplace, but often include Christian Spanish-language media contacts.

- **Hispanic Newswire**
  This service offers comprehensive distribution, sending releases to Spanish-language newspapers, magazines, radio, television, and websites in the United States.
  www.hispanicprwire.com

- **National Association of Hispanic Journalists (NAHJ)**
  The NAHJ is another resource for reaching journalists with Hispanic news and information.
  www.nahj.org

Spanish-Language Book Awards

Currently, the only Christian Spanish-language book awards are given by SEPA (Spanish Evangelical Products Association). Since almost all of the bestselling Spanish-language Christian titles are translated versions of bestselling English-language Christian books, many of the awards given by SEPA mirror ECPA's Christian Book Awards.

- **Spanish Evangelical Products Association (SEPA) Book Awards**
  These awards include the Harold Kregel Book of the Year Award, the Best Original Spanish Work of the Year Award, and Gallery of Honor Silver, Gold, and Platinum Awards based on sales figures for a title.
  www.sepaweb.org

There are a few Spanish-language book awards for the general book marketplace. One such award program has been implemented by Latino Literacy Now. While this program is not specifically geared toward Christian books, religious books can be submitted for consideration in the award categories offered.

- **International Latino Book Awards**
  These awards accept nominated titles from South, Central, and North America. Awards are given for children/youth, fiction, and nonfiction books and are presented each year at BookExpo America.
  www.lbff.us

Summary

The fundamentals of marketing Spanish-language books are the same as for English-language books. The challenge is in knowing how to reach Spanish readers. One good source for finding people to help you connect to Spanish-language readers is the Latina Book Club (www.latinabookclub.com). While this is not a Christian book club, their website has a number of resources for authors.

Part Four

Reference

Index

Suppose one of you wants to build a tower. Won't you first sit down and estimate the cost to see if you have enough money to complete it?
—Luke 14:28

Marketing Fundamental:
Providing your customers a quality experience creates loyalty.

advertising
   direct mail......................81-83
   distributor, through..................81
   e-newsletter, in....... 78, 81, 126, 180, 217
   magazines, in......................94
   online 153-156
   trade journals, in..................77-78
Amazon
   Author Central..................162-164
   Kindle Direct Publishing 195-196

associations
   benefits of...........................8
   camp & conference center 113-114
   Christian organizations 101-104
   collegiate......................108-111
      American Academy
         of Religion.............. 95, **109**, 110
      Association of
         Theological Booksellers........ 68, **110**
   digital publishing....................192

homeschool
  Homeschool Speakers
    and Vendors Association 218
  National Challenged Homeschoolers
    Associated Network..............208
library
  American Library
    Association.......... 36, **48**, 141, 230
  American Theological
    Library Association..............110
  Association of
    Christian Librarians.......... 49, **111**
  Catholic Library Association 48, **88**
  Church and Synagogue Library
    Association...................48, **89**
  Evangelical Church Library
    Association, The...............48, **89**
  military..........................104
  Pacific Northwest Association
    of Church Libraries...............89
  publications of...................48-49
media & press
  Associated Church Press, The.......121
  Catholic Press Association, The.....121
  Catholic Radio Association.........129
  Evangelical Press Association.......121
  National Association of
    Black Journalists..................225
  National Association of
    Black Owned Broadcasters........227
  National Association of
    Hispanic Journalists..............236
  National Newspaper Publishers
    Association, The.................224
  National Religious Broadcasters.....126
  Religion Newswriters Association...123
military........................103-104
publishers
  Alliance of Independent Authors......12
  Association of
    Catholic Publishers............**10**, 82
  Association of Publishers
    for Special Sales 11
  Christian Small
    Publishers Association .. **10**, 30, 52, 66
  Digital Book World 192
  Electronic Publishing
    Industry Coalition...............192
  Evangelical Christian
    Publishers Association **10**, 67
  Independent Author Network 12
  Independent Book
    Publishers Association **10**, 68, 199
  International Digital
    Publishing Forum 192

Protestant Church-Owned
  Publishers Association 10
Small Publishers, Artists,
  and Writers Network..............11
Spanish Evangelical
  Products Association........ **232**, 236
retail
  Association of
    Theological Booksellers....... 68, **110**
  CBA, The Association
    for Christian Retail 76, **82**, 83, 132
  Covenant Group...................79
  Episcopal Booksellers
    Association, Inc...................83
  Logos Bookstore Association........80
  Munce Group 76, **80**
  scholastic......................107-108
  seminary – see associations, collegiate
  Spanish-language............... 232, 236
  speakers......................135-136
  Urban 224-225, 227
writers
  American Christian Fiction
    Writers Association............**15**, 66
  American Christian
    Writers Association...............15
  Catholic Writers Guild..............15
  Christian Writers Guild.............15
  Fellowship of Christian Writers 15
  Small Publishers, Artists,
    and Writers Network..............11
awards
  Christian.......................65-68
  ebook.........................198-199
  general........................68-71
  Spanish-Language..............236-237
  Urban 229-230
BISAC................................75
blogs
  advertising on......................155
  blog tour..................160-162, 216
  blog tour services....................162
  carnival..........................173
  creating.......................171-173
  homeschool 216
  reviewers....................50-51, 216
book awards – see awards
book clubs – see also reading groups
  African American
    Literature Book Club 222
  Black Expressions 227
  Black Inspirations Book Club 227
  Good Girl Book Club 226
book fairs & festivals 139-140
  scholastic book fairs 105

Index | 243

Harlem Book Fair 222
Spanish-language. 232-233
book reviews – see reviews
book signings 132-133
  digital 203-204
book videos – see videos
booksellers associations – see associations
bookstores – see retailers
broadcast media - see radio and/or television
bundling 145, 196
catalogs
  chain store 79-81
  consumer catalogs....................84
  direct mail..........................141
  directory of mail-order catalogs 98
  homeschool 210-211
  mail-order catalogs 98-99, 210-211
  online search for **99**
  retail marketing group 79-80
  seasonal..........................79-81
  Theological Best Books...............110
Catholic resources
  Association of Catholic Publishers ...**10**, 82
  Association of Catholic
    Colleges and Universities............109
  Catholic Advertising Network.........121
  Catholic Child 99
  Catholic Library Association........48, **88**
  Catholic Library World.............48, 88
  Catholic Marketing Network........78, **79**
  Catholic Marketing
    Network Trade Show 76
  Catholic Online 157
  Catholic Press Association, The.... 66, **121**
  Catholic Press Awards.................66
  Catholic Radio and
    Television Network............ **129**, 235
  Catholic Radio Association 129
  Catholic Word Publisher Group 29
  Catholic Writers Guild 15
  CatholicFiction.net 51
  CMG Booking 136
  CMN Marketplace News 78
  CMN Seasonal Catalogs...............79
  Consolidated Mailing Services 107
  Homeschooling Catholic 209
  Mrs. Nelson's Book Fair Company 105
  National Catholic
    Education Association 108
  National Catholic College
    Admission Association, The 109
  National Federation for Catholic
    Youth Ministries, The................92
  Official Catholic Directory, The.......93, 94
  RBTE..............................75

cause marketing........................143
**CBA, The Association
  for Christian Retail** 76, **82**, 83, 132
CBA Retailers + Resources..... 13, 35, **43**, 78
chain stores – see retailers
Christian Books & More Database 34
Christian Retailing 13, 35, **44**, 66,
                                68, 78, 82, 233
church libraries................88-89, 93-94
conferences - see conventions
conventions
  camp and conference center 113
  Christian education..........88, 92-93, 108
  church leader 91-92
  education 92-93
  homeschool 209, 217-219
  industry trade shows...............75-77
  library 88-89, 110-111
  media............. 121, 122, 126, 224, 227
  pastor..............................95
  Spanish-language.................232-233
  speaking to 134-136, 218
denominations.. 87, **90-93**, 113-114, 135, 228
direct mailings......................81-83
  church card packs 93
  email campaigns 156-157
  email list management services........157
  homeschool card packs...............220
  mailing lists – see mailing lists
  press release services.... 122-123, 127-128,
                                      224, 236
discussion groups 14, 15, 16, 217
distribution
  bargain book companies..........184-186
  Christian distributors 28-29
  Christian wholesalers 26-27
  distributors vs. wholesalers 24-25
  ebook..........................193-198
  general market wholesalers 27
  homeschool 209-211
  library 141, 196-197
  print-on-demand..................30-31
  Spanish-language.................233-234
  Urban 222
  wholesalers vs. distributors 24-25
email campaigns 156-157
endorsements......................19-21
Facebook.......................173-174
foreign rights 143
free services
  BlogTalkRadio 164-166
  book video sites 159
  bookcrossing 146-147
  cable television......................130
  catalog search engine 99

Christian Books & More Database......34
Craigslist...........................167
ebook promotion................200-203
media connection...............123-124
online discussion groups... 14, 15, 16, 217
press release...................128, 157
speakers bureau listing..........136, 218
Goodreads.......................179-180
Google+.........................177-178
Hispanic – see Spanish-language
industry publications – see periodicals
lectures – see speaking
libraries see church and/or public
library associations – see associations
mailing lists
   camp & conference center............113
   CBA................................82
   Christian schools...............107-108
   church........................90-91, 93
   collegiate.......................110-111
   homeschool........................220
   library......................88-89, 141
   Religion Newswriters Association.....123
   retail stores........................82
   scholastic....................107-108
   seminary......................110-111
Midwest Book Review..................46
nonprofit groups.............100, 186-187
online discussion groups..... 14, 15, 16, 217
periodicals
   industry......................12-13, 35
   consumer.....................118-122
   homeschool..................213-214
   Urban.......................222-224
   Spanish-language...................236
   CBA Retailers + Resources ... 13, 35, **43**, 78
   Christian Retailing..........13, 35, **44**, 66,
                            68, 78, 82, 233
Pinterest.........................175-176
press releases.....................42-43
   sample..............................43
   services
      general.....................122-123
      free........................127-128
      Spanish-language................236
      Urban......................224-225
professional associations – see associations
promotional items...............144-145
public libraries..........140-142, 196-197
public speaking – see speaking
publishers associations – see associations
Publishers Portal
QR codes...........................166
radio
   BlogTalkRadio.................164-166

Christian radio and television.....124-130
   homeschool radio programs..........216
   list of stations.....................130
   press releases for...............127-128
   publicity services for...............126
   Spanish-language................235-236
   Urban.........................227-228
reading groups....................137-139
   Urban.........................226-227
retail associations – see associations, retail
retailers..............................
   bargain book companies..........184-186
   chain and franchise stores..........78-81
   homeschool....................211-213
   online..........................85-86
   retail marketing groups............78-81
reviews
   applying for.....................42-43
   blog...........................53, 160
   Christian trade...................43-44
   Church librarians............47-49, 87-88
   consumer..........49-50, 89-90, 119-120
   ebook reviews......................200
   general trade...................44-47, 53
   homeschool....................213-216
   online review sites................50-51
   social media and...............164, 172
   Spanish-Language...................233
   Urban.........................222-224
school book fairs - see book fairs
schools, Christian - see associations
services
   press release
      general.....................122-123
      free........................127-128
      Spanish-language................236
      Urban......................224-225
   linking journalists w/ experts.123-124, 126
social networking.................169-181
   Amazon Author Central..........162-164
   Facebook......................173-174
   Goodreads....................179-180
   Google+.......................177-178
   Pinterest.....................175-176
   Twitter.......................176-177
   blogging......................171-173
   book-focused sites..............178-180
   homeschool sites..............215-216
   online communities..................180
   rules of engagement.............170-171
   sites.........................173-180
   Urban.............................230
Spanish-language market...........231-237
speaking
   author speaking engagements.....134-136

church leaders' conferences 91-93
Friends of the Library 142
publicity services 135-136
speakers bureaus 135-136, 218, 225
    homeschool 218
    Urban 225-226
schools, speaking at 105-106
television
    cable television 130
    Christian television networks 129-130
    press releases for 127-128
    publicity services for 126
    Spanish-language 235-236
    Urban 227-228
trade shows - see conventions
Urban market 221-230
videos 157-159
Twitter 176-177
websties, creating 150-153
wholesalers – see distribution
writers associations – see associations

About the Author

SARAH BOLME is the Director of Christian Small Publishers Association (CSPA), the owner of CREST Publications, and the author of 7 books including the award-winning *Your Guide to Marketing Books in the Christian Marketplace,* and numerous articles. She is also the editor of the *CSPA Circular,* the monthly newsletter of Christian Small Publishers Association.

A clinical social worker by education and experience, Sarah stumbled into the world of publishing after her two self-help books were published by a small publisher. Sarah and her husband, a fiction author, then collaborated on a set of board books for infants and toddlers after the birth of their children. After much thought and research, they decided to publish the project themselves. This decision led to the creation of CREST Publications and Sarah's journey into marketing.

Navigating the Christian marketplace began as a rather solitary learning experience for Sarah as no guide books or associations were available for marketing in this unique marketplace. After meeting and dialoging with other small and self-publishers marketing books in the Christian marketplace, it became clear that an organization was needed to provide assistance and information to new and emerging publishers. Christian Small Publishers Association (CSPA) was founded in January 2004 with Sarah Bolme as Director.

Sarah's passion is educating others to help them improve their situation whether that is helping them get unstuck in their lives through counseling, learning and applying Biblical truths, or marketing their books into the Christian marketplace. Sarah conducts seminars for writers and publishers in the areas of publishing, marketing, and social media.

Home Page: www.marketingchristianbooks.com
Blog: http://marketingchristianbooks.wordpress.com
CSPA: http://www.christianpublishers.net
CREST Publisher Services: www.crestpub.com
Twitter: @SarahBolme

Sarah Bolme

Download Sarah's Book Marketing Template Companion

To help authors and publishers organize their marketing efforts leading up to and following the publication of a book, Sarah Bolme has developed a book marketing template designed to be used in conjunction with her book *Your Guide to Marketing Books in the Christian Marketplace*.

The template provides organization around activities that should be done:

- 6 months prior to publication
- 4 months prior to publication
- 2 months prior to publication
- The month of publication
- Ongoing promotional activities

The template can be purchased as an Excel Spreadsheet or in PDF format and reused as often as you like. Your cost is just $4.99.

Purchase your copy today at www.marketingchristianbooks.com!

Christian Small Publishers Association®

Join Now!

Get the help and support you need in marketing your book(s) to the Christian marketplace!

What We Do

Assist publishers and independently published authors in marketing books in the Christian marketplace.

Membership Eligibility

- You must be a small publisher or independently published author with revenues of less than $400,000 per year,
- You must publish materials for the Christian marketplace, and
- You must agree to abide by CSPA's code of conduct.

Membership Benefits Include

- Monthly e-newsletter packed with information on publishing and marketing books,
- BookCrash, a book review program,
- Christian Small Publisher Book of the Year Award,
- Cooperative marketing opportunities,
- Representation of members' products at the International Christian Retail Show (ICRS), and
- Discounts on products and services from our Partner Members.

To Apply

Applying is easy! Apply online on our website at www.christianpublishers.net.

Sarah Bolme

BOOKCRASH

A good book can change your world.

Become a BookCrash Blogger! Get Free Books!

Bloggers who review Christian books on their blogs can get **free books** from Christian publishers to read
—*in exchange for*—
Writing a fair review of each book received.

Here is how it works:

1. You sign up at bookCrash to become a reviewer.
2. BookCrash aproves you as a review blogger.
3. You browse the books available for review on BookCrash and request a copy of the book you are interested in reviewing.
4. You receive the book for free.
5. You read the book.
6. You write a 200-word fair review of the book and post it on your blog and one other consumer book site (such as Amazon.com or BarnesandNoble.com).
7. You send BookCrash the links to your review.
8. Repeat steps 3 through 7 as often as you like!

Sign up now at www.BookCrash.com!

―― *Sarah Bolme* ――

Get Your Special Marketing Bonus!

Thank you for buying the latest edition of *Your Guide to Marketing Books in the Christian Marketplace*.

In thanks for your support, you may scan this QR code in your phone or tablet and listen to an additional marketing tip from author Sarah Bolme.

P.S.: The QR codes at the start of each chapter also link to additional resources.